MUSIC OUTSIDE

Contemporary Jazz in Britain

"But if there may be death in commercial music, and in 'straight' music and in jazz no less, there may also be life in all three. We have merely to recognise the creative spirit whenever and wherever we may meet it; and this is why segregation of the genres, in our much divided and departmentalised society, is meaningful no longer, if ever it was meaningful."

WILFRID MELLERS
Music in a New Found Land

"The darkest despotisms on the Continent have done more for the growth, and elevation of the fine arts than the English government. A great musical composer in Germany and Italy is a great man in society, and a real dignity and rank are universally conceded to him. So it is with a sculptor, or painter, or architect. Without this sort of encouragement and patronage such arts as music and painting will never come into great eminence. In this country there is no general reverence for the fine arts; and the sordid spirit of a money-amassing philosophy would meet any proposition for the fostering of art, in a general and extended sense, with the commercial maxim — Laissez-faire."

S. T. COLERIDGE
Table-Talk

MUSIC OUTSIDE

Contemporary Jazz in Britain

IAN CARR

Second Edition

Published by Northway Publications
39 Tytherton Road, London N19 4PZ, UK.
www.northwaybooks.com

The publishers acknowledge with thanks the assistance of David Nathan
of the National Jazz Archive in the search for photographs and the kind
permission of copyright holders to reprint the images used in this book.
Permissions have been sought in all cases where the identity of the copyright holders is known.

Cover design based on original cover (first edition) by Keith Davis.

First published 1973 by Latimer New Dimensions Ltd.

This edition published 2008.

A CIP record for this book is available from the British Library.

ISBN 978 09550908 6 8

Printed and bound in Great Britain by Cromwell Press Ltd,
Trowbridge, Wiltshire.

CONTENTS

INTRODUCTION TO THE NORTHWAY EDITION

For this edition, Ian Carr's 1973 text and discography remain unchanged except for the correction of some minor errors. New photographs have been added, and a new postscript brings up to date some of the main themes of this classic book.

INTRODUCTION

In March 1972, Stan Tracey rang me up and asked me to go to a meeting he was organising to discuss the situation of jazz music and jazz musicians in Britain. During the course of the conversation, I asked him how he was doing himself and he replied: "Terribly! I've been on the dole so long that they want to retrain me for other work!"

To understand just how shocking this reply was, it is worth drawing comparisons with individuals in other arts. Tracey is a pianist in his middle forties, a complete master of his craft, one of the few really considerable and adult talents in Britain, with an astonishingly original mind which never ceases to explore . . . In fact there are few equivalents in other arts, or indeed in other branches of music, because most people simply find a formula and carry on working it out or working within it for the rest of their lives. But suppose, for instance, that Harold Pinter or the painter Richard Hamilton were on the dole and being pressurised to train as a clerk or bus conductor. In both cases the hypothesis is unthinkable. Yet here, in jazz, we have a man of proven high quality who is simply not valued. Worse still, Stan Tracey's predicament is nothing new among jazz musicians. Jazz is a music outside, a perpetual Cinderella of the arts in Britain, and in this introductory chapter I would like to demonstrate why.

It is not the fault of the music: contemporary British jazz is in a remarkably healthy condition. So many exceptionally gifted musicians are involved in it that there is more variety of conception and more sheer originality than ever before. And yet, though the rest of the world has been quick to recognise the new vitality of the British contribution, the British public and the cultural establishment — the media, schools, colleges, universities — remain almost entirely unaware of its quality and its international significance. General ignorance is understandable, for jazz is more or less ignored by the press, largely excluded from television, only minimally featured on radio, hardly ever forms part of the music syllabus at schools and colleges, and receives no official attention from the universities. But when we ask why exactly it is that jazz is thus culturally ostracised we can find a simple and pretty well conclusive

Ian Carr

answer in the mechanism for disseminating information about music that exists in Britain today.

The music establishment divides into two broad areas — 'popular' music, which is taken care of by big business, and 'serious' music, which is nourished by the state. Both, therefore, are heavily promoted by the mass-media, and besides television and press coverage, on BBC radio each area has virtually a whole channel to itself, Radio 1 promoting the pop/rock productions and Radio 3 'serious' music — which of course is also taught and studied in schools, colleges and universities.

A fair amount of British jazz has been recorded during the last six years or so, but as the records receive only minimal promotion, their existence for the most part is simply unnoticed by either the general public or the cultural establishment — in fact, more is known about them abroad than at home. In other words, big business will occasionally record a jazz group, but will not publicise the record in the way that pop, rock and 'serious' music are publicised. At the same time, contemporary jazz is almost completely excluded from Radio 1 and, at the time of writing, is given a mere thirty or forty minutes once a fortnight on Radio 3, and this on a Friday afternoon — a virtually inaccessible time for all except retired colonels and out-of-work musicians.

To become acceptable to either the pop/rock or the 'serious' areas of the music establishment, jazz has to be redefined in terms that are fundamentally alien to it . . . hence the entertainment angle of some trad bands which appear regularly on Radio 1 and on television, and the 'art' angle of some 'serious' avant-garde groups which, if they're lucky, might appear once a year on Radio 3. But both these angles falsify the true situation; jazz cannot be fitted into either category and remain true to itself. If one of the

main functions of true art is to question the values and
assumptions of society, then it is in this area that jazz must
be classed — and in the context of the second half of the
twentieth century this means questioning the validity of dis-
tinctions between 'high' and 'low' art, between entertainment and art, and between what is acceptable to a mass,
and what to an elite, audience.

The music, as I have said, is healthy, and more than
healthy; but its finances and its whole socio-cultural base
are both precarious and sick. Ironically, it has been subsidised and encouraged more by radio stations and the
mass media in other European countries where it is much
better understood by the cultural establishments, and
where the regular dissemination of information has helped
to create a considerable amount of public interest. The
enlightened German radio, for instance, unlike our own,
divides its music into three categories: light entertainment,
serious — and jazz.

Fortunately, there is something to be said on the credit
side. Remedies are being sought and tried, and though a
great deal of fighting is still to be done, there have been
enough small victories to bring an air of hope to the situation. For one thing, the Arts Council of Great Britain has
at last begun to show a strong and sustained interest in the
music. The first Arts Council grant to a jazz musician was
awarded to bassist Graham Collier in 1968 and, since then,
besides the fairly regular grants to individual musicians,
and the active encouragement of local arts centres to pro-
mote jazz events, grants have also been made to the Jazz
Centre Society, a charitable body — often and inevitably,
unfairly criticised — which was formed by devotees in 1968
to try to improve conditions for musicians and whose
efforts have time and again provided the only bulwark
against complete chaos and disintegration. Even so, jazz

still receives considerably less support from the Arts Council than do other types of music.

When Stan Tracey phoned me in March 1972, I resolved to go to the meeting he was organising, determined to become involved in whatever transpired; and it was at that meeting that the Musicians' Action Group was formed. It is a loosely organised affair with neither committee nor president; it aims to represent the interests of all musicians, specifically the interests of jazz and other improvising musicians, the worst served in our cultural setup. Its prime function is educative: to inform the various controllers of the media and the cultural moguls about jazz and jazz musicians — in other words, to get at the source of the widespread ignorance I have described.

During the first twelve months of its existence, MAG has obtained the backing and co-operation of the Musicians' Union, has had its first discussion with the controllers of the BBC, and has begun liaison with the recently formed (1973) House of Commons Jazz Society, a parliamentary lobby concerned with promoting the art.

Whatever the short-term results of the Musicians' Action Group, its primary importance is that, for the first time, a representative cross-section of British jazz musicians have got together in order to make a systematic attempt to improve their working conditions.

My purpose in writing this book can be seen to follow on from the aims of the MAG — that is, to provide some basic information about the current British jazz scene, to give some idea of the kinds of people involved in it, of the variety of their personalities and talent, and of the amount of their work already on record. I chose to interview and write in-depth chapters on several people — Mike Westbrook, John Stevens and Trevor Watts, Jon Hiseman, Evan Parker, Chris McGregor and Mike

Gibbs — because they seemed to represent important and very different areas of activity. These interviews took place during the latter half of 1972. But the book is, of course, not intended to be a comprehensive survey. I am very grateful to the musicians who were interviewed, and for their co-operation in reading through and correcting their own chapters. I have also taken the opportunity of describing my own experience and work with Nucleus — to give a first-hand account of what it has been like, and is, to be a jazz musician and leader of a group in Britain today.

I hope this information will give an idea of the relatively wide area of musical activity which now lacks and needs thorough documentation, study, and a detailed assessment of achievements — though in the assessing it would be wise to bear in mind these cautionary remarks by the French critic, André Hodeir:

> Anyone who tries to place jazz in the perspective of European culture without first revising his traditional artistic habits has scarcely any chance of understanding it. When an art involves the most elaborate forms of a culture, often only the most highly educated minds can grasp it. When an art is foreign to a culture, it seems, on the contrary, that greater educational conditioning can retard or even prevent an understanding of it. (André Hodeir, *Jazz: Its Evolution and Essence*, New York: Grove Press, 1956.)

1

PERSPECTIVES

A panoramic view of the jazz scene in Britain reveals extremes both of personality and types of musical activity. The precarious economics and the unsympathetic cultural climate make for a very high drop-out rate among jazzmen. More often than not, people who started playing in their teens and throughout their twenties were prepared to put up with the various privations — the arduous journeys, the small financial returns — begin, one by one, to succumb to the bitch-goddess of money and security as their first enthusiasm wanes. With the exception of a few, a very few, remarkable individuals, the majority of musicians by the time they're approaching forty have settled for some comfortable routine — regular session work in the studios perhaps; at any rate, some steady job. If they continue to be interested in jazz at all, it is as a sort of hobby rather like darts or golf, and, as a natural corollary, they are usually more interested in trying to recreate past experience than in trying anything new.

For the heroic few who do continue to be totally committed to the music after they have reached their forties, there is often a terrible price to pay. The saxophonist Joe Harriott and his long-time associate the drummer Phil Seamen both died in 1972. They were in their early forties. Phil Seamen was worn out by drug addiction, but Joe

Harriott, one feels, was defeated and worn down and out more directly by the system, the hostile environment. From being one of the leading pioneers of 'free' jazz, and the co-creator of the Indo-Jazz Fusions which made such an impact in the 1960s, for the last two years of his life he had been reduced to the obscurity of the provinces where he wandered about working as a soloist with local rhythm sections.

Saxophonist Tubby Hayes, one of the most robust talents Britain has ever produced, and one of her most famous musicians, did not even reach the age of forty: he died in June 1973, aged thirty-eight. Phil Seamen, Joe Harriott and Tubby Hayes were outstandingly gifted and internationally acclaimed for their work, yet all three were penniless when they died — a damning indication of how little jazz has been valued here.

Seen in this kind of harsh light, the survival and constant artistic development of Stan Tracey seems little short of miraculous. Tracey was one of the most individual and most vital musicians in Britain in the 1950s when he was pianist first with Laurie Morgan's Elevated Music, which played some of the lesser known and harder Thelonious Monk tunes, and later with the Ted Heath band. And in 1973, he is still one of the most daring and original musicians around — more so, if anything, since he has worked his way right through the early Monk influence and emerged with something all his own.

His development is fairly well documented on record, but can be seen more clearly in the small group albums than in his big band work. The main characteristics of his music are immense harmonic knowledge, a ferocious rhythmic sense, and a very dramatic use of space. In fact, he is a sort of Jackson Pollock of the piano, using the keyboard rather like an abstract expressionist painter uses a canvas-splashing colour on to it. It could be that once he has absorbed the new dimension of 'free' playing which he is currently exploring with John Stevens, Trevor Watts, and his own ten-piece band Tentacles, he may produce some of the most lasting work of our time. His quartet album *Under Milk Wood* (1965) is, of course, already a classic of British jazz.

Stan Tracey (photo Jazz Centre Society).

The amazing variety in jazz activity today, against all the odds, is due to the determined efforts of strong-willed individuals to create work for themselves and for others. Bassist Graham Collier, for example, has been able to keep his various bands together by sheer strength of character. He has gone out and looked for the work, and time after time his band has opened up new places to jazz — new festivals, new establishments, and indeed some key work areas abroad. He was the first British musician to have a concert of his own music with an international band at the Hamburg Jazz Workshop, the first young British composer to be invited to Denmark to conduct a performance of his music by the Danish radio orchestra. And, as I mentioned earlier, he was the first jazz musician to receive an Arts Council grant; this kind of pioneering is typical of him. A literate and articulate person, he can also explain his music to audiences — which, in a verbal culture like ours, can mean the difference between working and not working. As a result, he has done a great deal of playing (and explaining) in schools. And because he's interested in words he's done a fair amount of mixed-media work, writing for voice and using poetry and songs in some of his performances. At the moment he is also writing three books on jazz — a general introduction for the layman; a handbook for teachers (half historical and half practical), and a book of compositional devices, a textbook for students, which will be issued as a package, together with a set of scores, with his LP *Songs For My Father.*

Collier studied at the Berklee School of Music in the United States from 1961–63, and has been leading a sextet and various other groups in England ever since. The list of musicians who have played in his band reads like a *Who's Who* of contemporary British jazz. Nearly all of his sidemen have been poll-winners at one time or another: Mike

Graham Collier (photo Jazz Centre Society).

Gibbs, John Marshall, Karl Jenkins, Harry Beckett, John Taylor, Nick Evans and Stan Sulzman, to name just a few, have been members of Collier's group.

A similarly tough character is pianist Michael Garrick, who manages to lead a sextet with a stable personnel. The rhythm section is the old Rendell—Carr Quintet unit with Garrick himself on piano, Dave Green on bass, and Trevor Tomkins on drums, and the front line includes trumpeter/violinist Henry Lowther, vocalist Norma Winstone, and Art Themen on saxes and flute. Like Graham Collier, Michael Garrick too is highly literate — he has a degree in English literature, and you can't get much more literate than that. Garrick has said: "All kinds of people in education, from the humblest to the most exalted, want to know about jazz. But they have to be led in a suitable way — which is the educative art", and in fact, this particular art occupies a good deal of his time. He works regularly with his rhythm section for various education authorities, and sometimes takes his sextet into schools either to play concerts or to make music with the pupils and staff. It is in the extension of this kind of activity that one hope of improvement lies.

But this is only one side of his work. Garrick has kept his sextet together by devoting a lot of energy to broadening the social and artistic scope of jazz in all kinds of directions. Following the work of poet Christopher Logue with the Tony Kinsey Quintet in the 1950s, and the New Departures Jazz/Poetry Quintet — poets Pete Brown and Michael Horovitz with Stan Tracey, Bobby Wellins, Les Condon, Jeff Clyne and Laurie Morgan — in the early 1960s, Garrick teamed up with poet Jeremy Robson in 1961 to organise the first concert of poetry and jazz at the Royal Festival Hall, attended by 3,000 people. Afterwards, for several years, they continued to give fairly regular concerts all over the British Isles, thus taking this rather hybrid art form out of bohemia and into the lumpen bourgeoisie. At the same time, he was exploring the possibilities of uniting jazz with religion — even during the early and halcyon days of the Rendell–Carr Quintet, when everyone else was reading newspapers or pulp novels on the long journeys to gigs — or telling dirty stories — Garrick would be immersed in one of his many volumes of Rudolf Steiner. During the 1960s he wrote a series of works for jazz group and choir — predating Duke Ellington's — and one of the highspots of this particular activity was a concert of his *Jazz Praises* in St. Paul's Cathedral in 1968.

The music of both Michael Garrick and Graham Collier is on the whole quite accessible to audiences. They both favour recognisable melodies, and they both use most of the known jazz techniques — such as improvisation based on chord sequences or on scales, different time signatures, and passages of out-of-time playing. Michael Garrick seems to sum up the musical intention of both groups when he says of his own unit: "the jazz development of the group is headed towards more freedom based on stronger inner discipline regarding basic musical elements — time, harmony and melody. In this way, one can see no end to increasing possibilities of expression and form."

The saxophonist and flautist Bob Downes is another inveterate pioneer. He has opened up a whole new area of operation for jazz musicians by working in close co-operation with dance groups — the Ballet Rambert and the London Contemporary Dance Theatre in particular — and he has written and played the music for many contemporary ballets. His writing commissions have come not only from British institutions but from Europe as well — the Cologne Opera House, for instance.

Michael Garrick (photo Jazz Centre Society).

In many ways, Downes is a unique figure. His music has the direct emotional appeal of the central jazz tradition, but at the same time he is an indefatigable and radical experimentalist. And he'll use anything to make music. For example, when he was collaborating with the sound poet Lily Greenham, he accompanied one of her pieces on a typewriter — punching out various rhythms. As well as all the sounds he can extract from his instruments, he uses his own voice from time to time as part of his total means of expression — grunts, roars, yelps and yodels. 'Open Music' is what he calls his work and his group, and that's a fairly accurate description.

Composer Neil Ardley is that unusual phenomenon in jazz — a writer and, from time to time, a bandleader who is not an instrumentalist, though he has a working knowledge of the piano. But then almost everything about him is unorthodox. He took a degree in chemistry at Bristol University, but earns his living as a freelance editor and writer for various publishers. When he first came to

London, because of his growing interest in music, he took over the leadership of that vitally important institution the New Jazz Orchestra, a band which was formed in about 1963 and stayed together as an intermittent unit throughout the 1960s. It was a band of player-composers, its express purpose to perform the works of new writers, and so it became a crucible for some of the strongest talents of the British scene. Apart from Neil Ardley himself, people as diverse as Mike Gibbs, Jack Bruce, Mike Taylor, Howard Riley, either wrote for or played in the NJO, or did both.

Ardley is one of the very few people to have written successful extended compositions incorporating improvisation. Although his musical background was the jazz tradition, and he was strongly influenced by Duke Ellington and Gil Evans, his methods of composition are more related in terms of structure and thematic development to the 'straight' music tradition than to jazz. The more he writes, the larger become the ensembles he writes for and the smaller the improvised sections. In fact it looks as if his tendency is away from improvisation altogether and towards totally written works. As well as writing for conventional instruments, he has collaborated with Keith Winter in the use of electronics, for a suite called *The Time Flowers* based on the science fiction story 'The Garden of Time' by J. G. Ballard.

At the other end of the jazz spectrum — away from large scored ensembles — there has been a strong movement since the end of the '60s towards the very personal totally improvised music of the duo. It seems to have begun in 1966 when the Spontaneous Music Ensemble was reduced to John Stevens on drums and Evan Parker on saxophone. Parker has since functioned as a duo with drummer Paul Lytton. Other duos active on the scene are

AMM — saxophonist Lou Gare and drummer Eddie Prevost — and a couple of musicians who call themselves Rain in the Face (Paul Burwell, drums, and David Toop, guitar, flutes). Playing as a duo involves its own austere discipline in which silence is often an integral part of the performance, and this new tradition is gradually building up its own musical vocabulary and atmosphere.

British jazz has recently developed to the point where a fair number of virtuoso players are capable of leading their own bands as well as working as sidemen for other leaders. Trumpeters Harry Beckett and Henry Lowther have both led their own groups; so have pianists John Taylor, Mike Pyne, Pat Smythe and Pete Lemer, and drummers Tony Oxley and Alan Jackson. Though there are still very few female jazz instrumentalists, saxophonist Barbara Thompson not only holds her own as a soloist but has been leading her own bands for two or three years now. In spite of the great difficulties that face the jazz musician in Great Britain, one of the most remarkable and heartening things is the reasonably steady stream of new young players — trumpeters like Marc Charig and Dick Pearce, pianists like Frank Roberts, Pete Saberton, Phil Broadhurst, Geoff Castle, saxophonists like Stan Sulzman, Elton Dean and Alan Wakeman, trombonists like Nick Evans. And these are only a fraction of the talented rising generation of players who will, in their turn, become frustrated and embittered unless there is a real improvement in living and working conditions for jazz musicians in the foreseeable future.

The National Youth Jazz Orchestra, run by the indefatigable Bill Ashton, and the annual jazz course at the Barry Summer School, have played a strong part in promoting interest in jazz among young people. The jazz course was started in 1966 by composer Pat Evans because he wanted

Keith Tippett
(photo Jazz Centre
Society).

to learn more about jazz himself and couldn't find any
institution to teach him. He negotiated with Glamorgan
Education Authority and they agreed to include jazz in
their summer school. Most of the young musicians listed
above have attended it, and it was there that the prodi-
giously talented pianist, Keith Tippett, first emerged as a
bandleader. That was in the late sixties; by 1970 he had
conceived, written for, and organised his gargantuan fifty-
piece orchestra Centipede. With all its faults — and it has
been severely criticised — the whole Centipede venture was
a quite astonishing feat of imagination, and a very coura-
geous effort on Tippett's part to draw together and fuse the
various strands of his musical experience to date. The
music combined elements from jazz, rock, and 'straight'
music, and the instrumentation included an amplified
string section as well as four vocalists, the usual big band
brass and reed sections, and a battery of percussion.

Another sign of the beginnings of cultural acceptance is
that the Leeds College of Music now has a permanent jazz
course, and, incidentally, one of the tutors is Pat Evans.

2

NOTES ON SOME VIRTUOSI

In jazz the key people are the virtuoso instrumentalists who improvise their compositions, and the visionary leaders and organisers (like those I have described and those who discuss their work in the following chapters) who create the stimulating contexts and playing conditions. I should like to add a few notes here on five virtuosi, to give some idea of the fascinating variety, the unlikely paradoxes of their personalities.

John Surman is unusual in combining the roles of visionary and virtuoso, and it is this dual function that has made him such an important figure in the British scene — he has not only made marvellous music himself, but has also inspired and encouraged many other musicians.

While Surman spent most of the 1960s in close collaboration with Mike Westbrook (see Chapter 3), he also fitted in three years of study at the London College of Music (1962–65) and a further year at London University for a Diploma in Education. This wide range of musical experience, from the pioneering jazz workshops with Westbrook to the orthodox academic world, has given him a strong sense of perspective and balance which, coupled with the international recognition he has received, has given him a poise and an air of authority rare among British musicians.

After he was voted best soloist at the Montreux Festival

of 1968, Surman began to make an impact all over the world as a baritone player. The American magazine *Downbeat* — the hip jazz enthusiast's bible — gave him a favourable mention in 1970, and in the *Downbeat* critics' poll he was to be voted first in the baritone section, an unprecedented honour for a British jazz musician.

In 1969 he left the Westbrook band to form his own trio with two Americans, bassist Barre Phillips and drummer Stu Martin — exacting playing conditions, but it was characteristic of his creative and physical stamina that he could survive, even thrive on them. And from 1968 to 1972 he simply wore out his passport travelling, both with and without the trio, all over Western Europe and Scandinavia, through the Iron Curtain to Poland, Czechoslovakia, Hungary and East Germany, to America and as far as Japan (where, representing Britain at the Japanese Expo '72, he was the only jazz musician not to be invited as a guest to his national stand — further evidence, if any more were needed, of British anti-jazz prejudice).

Then, bearing out Blake's proverb "The road of excess leads to the palace of wisdom," he suddenly left the road after four years non-stop travelling, left the trio and retired to his house in Kent. Though he still makes occasional trips abroad, he has turned his attention to the state of jazz in Britain — and in particular in Kent — and spends a good deal of time writing music, something almost impossible to do while he was permanently on the move. Having lived with the baritone saxophone night and day for several years, he now rarely plays it and concentrates rather on the soprano saxophone and bass clarinet.

Kenny Wheeler, though not primarily a leader, has played just as vital a part in the developing British scene. A glance through discographies will show the extent of his contribution to all facets of jazz. His compositions for small groups and very big bands are as distinguished as his improvising — the main hallmark of his writing, apart from his highly refined harmonic and rhythmic sense, is the creation of dense textures with the use of multiple and interdependent

Kenny Wheeler (photo Jazz Centre Society).

lines. For instrumental technique, power of thought and fertility of ideas he has few equals in the world today. His musical personality is so immensely strong that whatever context he is playing in — mainstream, bebop or the most austere avant-garde music — he is still instantly recognisable; and yet, paradoxically, he's an extremely shy person, undermined by self-doubt, showing none of the confidence his playing expresses. In fact, there are all kinds of apocryphal stories about his nervousness: when he was working with one of the first John Dankworth big bands, for instance, he is supposed to have been so terrified by the idea of a broadcast that he regularly used to send someone to deputise for him — though he needed the money.

Even today, having proved his worth a thousand times over, having won polls and gained an international reputation, he still has to fight his nerves. He once said: "I wouldn't mind playing badly if I could just relax and enjoy blowing!"

Gordon Beck at the Roundhouse, London, 1979 (photo © Jak Kilby).

Equally highly strung, and perhaps even more complex as a personality, is the pianist Gordon Beck. His first important professional job was with the Tubby Hayes Quintet at the beginning of the '60s, and since then, apart from working with various other British groups, he has led his own trio which included Jeff Clyne on double bass and Tony Oxley on drums. In the later 1960s he joined the Europe-based quartet led by the American alto saxophonist, Phil Woods, and this began a period of about four years of playing abroad. Phil Woods chose the members of his group with political as well as musical insight. The bass player was originally the large and bearded Frenchman Henri Texier (when he left, his place was taken by our own Ron Matthewson), and the drummer, the Swiss Daniel Humair. Woods chose the kind and the amount of work he wanted to do with similar care, with the result that, virtually overnight, Gordon Beck found himself elevated to VIP status. For the first time his talent seemed to receive the kind of steady recognition it deserved. He would spend most of his time at his home in West London, and then fly off for a short tour or a festival. A few days, and perhaps a few thousand miles, later he'd be back at home. It seemed the ideal arrangement and, while it lasted, Beck was almost happy.

For Gordon Beck is notorious for his apparently total pessimism. He seems to be in a constant state of despair about the selfishness and depravity of human nature, the sickness of the consumer society, the frailty of the whole economic structure of the West and its apparent imminent collapse. In personal and private terms, he fears the worst about everything — his own health, his own likelihood (or anyone else's for that matter) of getting to a concert on the right day — let alone at the right time. Whatever disaster might befall any man at any moment, you can be sure it will have been imagined by Gordon Beck. His inner tensions express themselves in a compulsive stream of commentary and surmise. Sitting in a plane waiting for take-off, he will ruminate aloud on recent air crashes, metal fatigue, pilot fatigue, and charred bodies. Once in the air he will hold up a hand, saying: "Look at my hand! It won't stop shaking! Nothing I can do about it. Now *why* is the pilot throttling down just as we approach the *Alps?* . . . Did you feel that *lurch?* He had to *swerve* to avoid that plane over there! . . . Do you know why I'm afraid of death? . . . Because I'm afraid of *life*, that's why!"

And yet, as soon as he starts to play the piano he gives the lie to his own gloom, because his playing is full of joy — is, in fact, a celebration of being alive. The brilliant and unquenchable flow of ideas and the superabundant technique express nothing less than jubilation.

Saxophonist Alan Skidmore seems on the surface to be the complete opposite. Where Beck is fastidious, hypertense and controlled, Alan Skidmore gives the impression of being gargantuan in his appetites, a roaring boy whose feelings are only just under control. All aspects of his appearance and behaviour are characterised by the same uninhibited flamboyance. In Italy with Nucleus he would shatter the sophisticated decorum of bourgeois Italian hotels with ear-splitting blasts on a referee's whistle which he wore round his neck. When he's not wearing the whistle, he lets out the occasional wild yell. Either way, the effect is the same.

I found it difficult to understand Alan Skidmore, until I came to realise, first, that his feelings really are so powerful that they have to be expressed and relieved, and, secondly, that he is an extremely sensitive and aware person. Perhaps it is the tension between these extremes that gives his playing such great strength. Apart from his work with his own quintet and with many other groups, he has also had a strong influence on the development of both Mike Westbrook's and Mike Gibbs' music. His technique and stamina are formidable, but perhaps his most memorable and catalytic quality is the immense warmth he emanates. Mike Gibbs says about him:

> In my band, he's one of the two extroverts. When we have a rehearsal and he isn't there, there seems to be little communication between me and the members of the band. When he arrives it's like the pin of the hand-grenade is pulled out and it comes to life!

There are very few musicians — perhaps none at all — whose activities are as wide-ranging as those of multi-reed player Tony Coe. He plays regularly with various mainstream groups, with contemporary big bands such as the Kenny Clarke–Francy Boland band of which he is a permanent member, with his own small group which he co-leads with Kenny Wheeler (Coe, Wheeler & Co.), and

Left to right: John Surman, Mike Osborne, George Khan, and Alan Skidmore.

with other units led by his contemporaries. He is also a permanent member of the 'straight' music ensemble, Matrix, led and organised by another virtuoso clarinettist, Alan Hacker. Sophisticated, gentle and vague, Tony Coe has an air of general abstraction as if he is perpetually trying to recall something he has forgotten. So far as music is concerned, the impression is deceptive: whatever he does, it is with total concentration and an intelligence which is at home with all types of musical activity.

These are just a few of the leading British virtuosi, and they all have a full understanding of the whole broad jazz tradition. In other words, their virtuosity is not just instrumental — it is also a stylistic, imaginative virtuosity. They are musicians with immensely strong individuality, but at the same time they are extremely flexible and can adapt to different contexts easily without losing their identity. Their talents have been, and are, crucial to the whole spectrum of developing British jazz.

3

MIKE WESTBROOK

Mike Westbrook's work has never fitted into the usual easy pigeonholes, and because he's always had the courage to change tack whenever he felt it necessary, he's set musicians and enthusiasts a lot of problems. The conventional jazz terms 'avant-garde', 'mainstream', ' bebop', etc simply cannot be applied to his work; what he does is pure Westbrook and beyond any form of simple categorisation.

Just because his work is so very demanding, it has, time after time, exposed the poverty of British jazz criticism which seems to specialise in over-praise or over-blame. Westbrook has suffered from frequent misleading bracketing with Duke Ellington. Hailed by some critics as 'the new Duke Ellington', he has at the same time been viciously attacked by others who accused him of having few of the Duke's virtues, both sides missing the essential and elementary point that it is irrelevant to judge Westbrook as if to copy or emulate Ellington were his only purpose. Westbrook is neither competing with him nor trying to follow in his footsteps; in fact, one way of coming to an understanding of Westbrook's work is to find out first of all where he differs from the Duke.

For me, an important key to his continuing development and his perpetual and confusing tendency to shoot off at a tangent lies in a statement he made a few years ago:

John Surman (*left*) and Mike Westbrook during the recording of
Westbrook's album *Citadel/Room 315*, 1975 (photo Kate Westbrook).

"I may be discovering things that people have known
about for years, but I'm discovering them for myself."

In his life, as well as in his music, he seems to have
worked things out — often painfully — by trial and error.
He began to be interested in music at school, when his
prime concern was painting. Even so, it wasn't until he'd
wasted a year as an articled clerk to an accountant, two
years doing National Service and a year at Cambridge
studying geography, that he realised that what he really
wanted was to concentrate on painting. And then, during
the three years he spent at Plymouth Art School, he began
to realise that music was perhaps his first love.

What sets Westbrook apart from most other jazz musicians, in fact, is his highly developed visual sense. The way
he describes the first jazz concerts he went to shows his
awareness and enjoyment of the spectacular side of the
music. He was very taken by the organised theatricality of
the big band shows:

The musical fare of that time was mainly big bands. Eric Delaney's band, for instance, had those marvellous trumpet players who used to scream away in the upper register . . . they had this drum kit which revolved on a platform which was an illuminated drum . . . There was a ballroom called The Spa . . . one of those real old Victorian places with lots of space. There was a bar and a great ballroom with lots of glitter. Ted Heath's band, in its prime, would do a fortnight or a month's residency there . . . They did an absolutely fabulous entertainment . . . all the aspidistras and the palms and the three singers sitting by the stage and getting up and doing their bit, and comedy routines with Johnny Hawksworth and Ronnie Verrell . . . It was the era when it was obligatory for every band to do *Skin Deep* and that was very exciting when everyone stopped dancing and watched the drummer.

And a year or two later, he went to a concert given by the Lionel Hampton band in Bournemouth:

I was sitting behind the band. Hampton himself was fantastic. He had his other drum kit which he played in front of the stage. Then he did this thing where he and the tenor player went around the audience, the tenor player squealing away and Hampton juggling about with drumsticks. And the band was roaring all the time . . . the whole stage was littered with cases and clothes. The band had obviously just flung themselves onstage and started playing. Every now and then the drummer would leap off his kit and kick all the rostrums together. It was obviously all sliding away . . . Then Hampton used to play those beautiful tunes on vibes like *Midnight Sun, High and Mighty* — things like that.

Westbrook had learnt the rudiments of the piano from his mother who was a piano teacher, though after going to a concert by the Humphrey Lyttelton band he got hold of a second-hand trumpet and played that for a while. In the same casual way, he found himself writing original compositions:

I used to spend a lot of time messing about on the piano trying to learn about chords and things which I still didn't know
. . . I used to like George Shearing at that time and I bought
some song copies of those tunes which are hellish complicated, and I'd struggle through very slowly playing all those
chord shapes which he did . . . and I did that with other song
copies, and when I saw how the chords started to move I'd
immediately start to improvise and make a few changes here
and there and before I knew, I'd wind up with an original
tune. So I got rather hooked on this idea of writing original
tunes.

While he was at art school, Westbrook got a sort of jazz
workshop going in Plymouth Arts Centre. He played there
constantly, writing arrangements for a four-piece front line
— which included John Surman on baritone. Surman was
sixteen at the time and still at school; but this was the beginning of an enormously fruitful relationship that was to last
about ten years, Surman developing into the poll-winning
instrumental virtuoso with a world reputation, and
Westbrook, never a virtuoso ("I'm a composer really and
an adequate piano-player. That's what my position in life
seems to be"), into a composer on the scale of the epic big
band works and multi-media events of the later '60s.

Because Britain is still, so far as the arts are concerned,
a one-city country, musicians deeply committed to jazz
usually try to get to London. Most of them arrive in the
metropolis with a job to go to or at least with some contacts
who might help them. Westbrook and Surman, some time
in the early '60s, with characteristic boldness tried to make
it with a completely unknown eleven-piece band. After a
period of intense scuffling, playing interval spots in clubs
and pubs for nothing, and trying to set up their own concerts and organise their own publicity, the strain proved
too much and the band broke up. Out of the remnants,

Ronnie Scott (photo Jazz Centre Society).

Westbrook formed his first sextet which included Surman on baritone, Mike Osborne on alto sax, Malcolm Griffiths, trombone, Harry Miller, bass, and Alan Jackson on drums. Shortly afterwards, Westbrook went back to Plymouth for the summer and more jazz workshops with Surman:

I spent one summer with John Surman down in Plymouth with a local bass player and drummer. And we began to find a whole new way of playing — the kind of thing which is now commonplace like free cadenzas resolving into rhythmic things and open-ended solos which could go on for ever. And that started to get translated into bigger groups. With the sextet we eventually got a broadcast and that was the first time I ever met or heard John Stevens, Paul Rutherford, Trevor Watts and co.

For young musicians the most essential thing is to play together as much as possible. Unknown rock musicians have less difficulty in getting regular playing experience because there are innumerable business organisations which will invest time and money in finding them work. They may be paid very little but at least they are playing, and there is always the feeling that if they do make an impact on audiences they may find themselves in the big-time and earning a fortune. For jazz musicians the situation is very different. There are absolutely no business organisations in the UK interested in jazz because, at the moment, there are no huge profits to be made from it. So for Westbrook and his associates the first problem was not how to earn a living by playing music, it was how to be able to play together enough to make the sextet a cohesive unit, and to enable it to develop its identity. This problem was at last partially solved when in 1966 John Stevens started organising late sessions at the Little Theatre Club (see Chapter 4). Each night of the week was given over to a group of musicians who had nowhere else to play, and for the first time the younger generation of musicians had a focal point — something to work for. This laid the foundations for what was to become a vital British jazz scene. And some months later playing facilities were further extended when the Ronnie Scott Club moved from its old premises in Gerrard Street. The lease of the old club had not expired, and Ronnie Scott offered the use of the premises to the rising generation of players. This became known as the Old Place, and it ran for eighteen months or so before the lease ultimately expired and it was forced to close down. These two venues — The Little Theatre Club and the Old Place — changed the whole climate of the British scene. Westbrook describes the importance of being able to play at the Old Place:

> Every Saturday night we played the all-nighter for about eighteen months. That was a fantastic thing and at first it was a real struggle to make it because we'd never done such a heavy gig. And in the early days of the Old Place there was a tremendous feeling — it was packed out and you really had to make it. Somehow we did. We discovered the energy and the groove. I think really it was the only time in my career that a band has had the opportunity to fulfil itself. Even then we couldn't earn a living. We got something like a fiver each for playing all night . . . All through the period at the Old Place I was earning my living by teaching art. My life was totally destroyed by that in a way. It had its good points but it meant, inevitably, that I spent every weekend either play-

ing or asleep or too tired to do anything. It made it very difficult for me personally. And it was the period when everything decided to happen. All the opportunities suddenly emerged at a time when I was at full stretch. I had a responsible job, young family and everything . . . but at the Old Place one heard for the first time what was going on on the scene . . . Like I heard Chris McGregor's band and various other musicians, and suddenly there was a British jazz scene and it had a focal point, and I think it's a tragedy that even that was under-appreciated . . . if this country is going to deserve a jazz scene then the audiences have got to get off their arses . . . I think they've got a lot to answer for!

So far as public support — audience size — was concerned, the Old Place followed a pattern which has become depressingly familiar on the jazz scene. In its early stages, the place was packed, but when the novelty wore off the audiences began to dwindle until eventually a full house was the exception rather than the rule. And, also typically, when it became known that the Old Place was about to be closed, attendances began to pick up.

However, during the eighteen months of the Old Place's existence, Westbrook's sextet began to make a reputation for itself and this was enhanced when the band was sent by the BBC to take part in the international competition at Montreux. The jury, which is always made up of extremely knowledgeable critics and jazz enthusiasts drawn from several European countries, voted John Surman to be the outstanding soloist of the competition.

As his reputation grew, Westbrook began to be offered occasional concerts outside London, and sometimes for a reasonable fee. When the finances permitted it, he started to think in big band terms again, and this was the beginning of the period which produced the series of epic extended works: *Celebration, Marching Song, Release, Metropolis,*

Earthrise. And this body of work, probably more than anything else, was responsible for the emancipation of British jazz from American slavery. At the beginning of the 1960s the British scene consisted mainly of a small, hip core of America-orientated musicians, who wore neat suits, were totally unflamboyant, and despised pop music. They also saw themselves in very rigid musical contexts — not only was there no meeting-point musically with pop, there was also a conscious avoidance of the jazz of the past. In 1960 a 'modern' jazzman was exactly that . . . a man who had left traditional jazz behind. But Westbrook was discovering or rediscovering the whole jazz tradition for himself, he was interested in the theatrical side of performance, regarded the audience as an integral part of any event (the hip jazz musician tended to try and ignore the audience), and he didn't want to be restricted by dogma or stylistic conventions. Also, for Westbrook, progress wasn't just a matter of going forward, it was a matter of following his nose and moving anywhere — backwards, sideways, up or down. The first inkling of what was to come was his composition *Celebration:*

> I had the opportunity to do a gig at Liverpool for a bit more bread than usual and I felt the yearning to do a big band thing again, so I got arrangements together and co-opted a few more musicians that I'd met at the Old Place. It was a twelve-piece band and we played *Celebration* which was like something that had been gestating for some time — the idea of doing a big suite that lasted the whole evening, accepting the fact that an evening at a club or a concert is a dramatic experience. It's not just a question of musical fragments, but whatever people play it's a theatrical experience for the listener and the participant really. I used to get this feeling going to concerts anyway. I felt that one should take this responsibility for the programming of things so that they

resolved in a meaningful way somehow, some kind of total experience. *Celebration* was the first attempt at that.

Celebration was totally acceptable to Westbrook's musicians — it fitted in easily with their ideas of what jazz was all about. It was also very well received by audiences, so it seemed that the big band events could be financially viable. But another factor made Westbrook eager to increase the size of his band occasionally: he was deeply impressed by the musicians he was hearing for the first time at the Old Place, and he wanted to be more closely associated with them:

> The only way was to write material that could involve these people . . . I had a big gig coming up in Plymouth for another arts festival. I'd written a piece called *Marching Song* some time before which was quite a simple frame-work, all about war and so on and derived from a sort of dream and nightmare situation. I'd toyed with a colossal big band version of it and in fact we'd even had a couple of rehearsals at the Little Theatre Club. But I wasn't together enough with the arrangements at that time. I went away and worked on it and I'd given myself this deadline — the arts festival. As it got nearer, of course, the usual thing happened. I had to decide what musicians I was going to use almost before I knew how I was going to use them . . . Eventually I took a few days off school, feigned sickness, and wrote the thing . . . and it was one of the great experiences of all time for me. We rehearsed bits of it and then had one all-night rehearsal at the Old Place. We went through the whole thing. There was nobody there but us and it was incredible! . . . We realised the depths that were in this thing and it was frightening! We did it at Plymouth and the London debut was the St. Pancras Festival the following year. The St. Pancras *Marching Song* which was very well attended and had every member of the press there was the turning point in a way. That

was where such notoriety as I've had as a big band leader was established, because they all wrote and raved about it the following day. Well, I don't mind because I thought it was good myself.

The relationship between a jazz composer and the musicians who work with him is a very delicate and subtle affair. He chooses his musicians because he likes the way they play — in other words he likes the way they compose by improvising — and one of his main problems is to produce musical contexts within which the musicians can freely express themselves. It is also essential that the musicians can identify in some way or other with his conception. Already with *Marching Song* there were signs of strain from this point of view:

> Although it was a fantastic period and I wasn't aware of any lack, I think I was suppressing certain things. Once I'd done *Celebration* and *Marching Song*, I realised it was possible to extend the kind of areas we were working in because I was doing things I'd never done before like brass band arrangements incorporated in the jazz thing and so on. I know it's all customary now, but at the time musicians would say — "Well, what the fuck is this?" Now they would accept it more readily, but in those days people fell about laughing when we played the march in *Marching Song* at the first rehearsal. I think they saw the point. But I started to feel confidence and I thought, well, I had all sorts of whims about what I wanted to write and I never dared do them. For one thing, working in the Old Place you're in a very hip scene. You had to kind of watch your step in a way. I don't know where the pressure came from, but certainly there was this feeling. There was a certain kind of thing that was hip and OK. I think we were quite original within it, but one didn't play *Take the A Train* or *Flying Home* or something. . . It seems silly now, but at that time it was not easy to see room for a wider range of material. And one certainly didn't

play pop songs in a jazz context. I liked all these things and
there was no way for me to do anything about it.

The way out of this dilemma was actually suggested by
certain elements in the huge *Marching Song* band which
included musicians from all facets of the jazz spectrum and
one or two players whose experience had already cut
across the artificially purist boundaries between different
kinds of music:

> By doing *Marching Song*, suddenly I had George Khan in
> the band and he's one of those people who can't be classi-
> fied, but he was certainly well into pop and rock music . . .
> and Paul Rutherford who, although he's a free-jazz player,
> has Beatles records at home and Bob Dylan and things
> whereas everybody else has Miles Davis. Gradually I took
> my courage in both hands and wrote this thing called
> *Release*. I decided right, any tune that I fancy I'm going to
> do, for whatever reason . . . Then I remembered *Flying
> Home*, Lionel Hampton, and I thought this is fantastic
> music, I don't see why we shouldn't play it. So I got togeth-
> er this small ten-piece concert band with Dave Holdsworth,
> Paul Rutherford, Malcolm Griffiths, Mike Osborne, John
> Surman, George Khan, Bernie Living, Harry Miller and
> Alan Jackson . . . and I wrote *Release* which incorporated
> free collective improvisation, collective improvisation over
> changes, blues and ballads, marches, old standards, the old
> saxophone chorus out of *Flying Home*, funky bits and bits
> where it was just a question of one instrumentalist playing
> on his own and leading into something else. *Girl from
> Ipanema* we played in absolutely authentic dance band style
> and that immediately resolved into complete cacophony.
> We had four rehearsals for it which was very unusual and I
> could see the band nudging each other and saying, "Christ!
> What's this?" But I think it's a tribute to the band that they
> eventually cottoned on and in the end they even used to
> enjoy it. I'd even overhear them practising *Flying Home*. So

when the thing eventually came in front of the public we also did a bit of presentation, like I painted a backdrop for the stage and the whole thing was a very slick sequence of things even though it was very loose . . . I don't know whether people cottoned on to what was happening or not, but it seemed to me that it was all building up to something and it was using the whole range of music or anything that I understood. There was quite a lot of humour in it which is important, and I think that these things ask questions of the people listening and of oneself like "What am I doing? Why am I here? What's it all about?". . . One got involved with this more sort of dramatic concept, what I think in a way is more a sort of poetry than music, just using images, sound images and exploiting the fact that certain sounds have certain associations which the listener can recognise at once. It may be something that they hate or it may be something that they secretly like . . . it may be passages of sheer noise. This all seemed important to me and still does.

With *Release*, Westbrook's whole conception of the drama of performance was beginning to extend and deepen. To the theatrical/narrative elements of the music and the growing obsession with sound images were now added the exploitation of personal relationships of musicians in the band and all the tensions and internal dramas they produced; at the same time he saw the band's relationship with audiences as an increasingly active phenomenon. The whole idea of a performing band and a passive, receiving audience was rapidly disappearing altogether. The germs of this development began before *Release* was written:

I remember we had one gig at Loughborough and I'd written out a few rock and roll riffs, although I don't think we thought of it as rock and roll: things like *A Piece of Mind* which comes at the end of *Release*. It was a 12/8 sort of pop thing – the sort of thing the Platters used to do, slow and with just a vamp. And we sort of threw ourselves on the stage and played these things and there were bits of free improvisation in between, complete chaos, and the audience was very irate. A very weird sort of agro was going on. But I was very excited by that evening . . . musicians were leaving the stage not wishing to be associated with what was going on. It was a weird, explosive situation with a bunch of characters with really incredible personalities, and all quite convinced about their own thing which was what the appeal was.

In fact, Westbrook was actually beginning to enjoy stirring things up — partly because to offend people's ideas of convention is a way of questioning deeply entrenched attitudes, and partly because he simply enjoyed the resulting furore. An ideal opportunity for his image-bashing iconoclasm occurred at the jazz poll-winners' concert at the Festival Hall in 1968. After *Marching Song* his big band had been voted into first place in the *Melody Maker* Poll, but Westbrook had already moved on to *Release* and another area of exploration:

> John Dankworth was on backing Cleo Laine earlier in the evening with his big band. We were waiting around backstage getting drunk. By that time the band had got wilder and my choice of material had got more extreme . . . It was doing more old ballads, and the free bits were even more violent and there were more pop songs . . . A lot of it was impudence I know on my part, chancing my arm really. I even sang, which was possibly a terrible mistake although it seemed to be the feature that all the critics noticed on that particular evening. But it was almost desperation because I hated that scene so much there. By the time we went on stage, in a way I didn't care, and in a way also I wanted to do something really strong. That was again heard by a lot of people and a lot of people hated it because it was nothing like any big band that had ever won the poll in the history of it. There was none of the neat suits and all that kind of business at all . . . just a band of individual people who were

drawn together by something, not in fact colossal respect in all cases but partly for some kind of thing that was alive. I think this is very important. I quite like it when the band's on stage playing and there are things going on inside — conflicts and moments of tension and real anger even at the way things are going.

Although he was cocking a snook at the whole big band tradition Westbrook still felt the need to prove himself in accordance with conventional big band criteria. Jazz musicians who develop in fundamentally improvising situations have often felt slightly uneasy when faced with the precision-playing of studio bands. And there is always a nagging worry that the artist may outstrip the craftsman . . . that dreams may not be expressed or may be botched simply because the artist does not have enough craftsmanship to convey them. Today jazz craftsmanship — the familiarity with existing techniques — is, on the whole, better than it has ever been, and at the core of the scene we have many musicians who have a profound and detailed knowledge not only of their instruments but also of writing techniques. The most outstanding example is Kenny Wheeler, a trumpet soloist of genius, a superb section-player, and an immensely subtle writer who can exploit all the resources of very big ensembles. In the heyday of the Old Place's life, Westbrook was worried about his own craftsmanship:

> I gave a little bit of encouragement to myself by plucking up the courage to write a conventional big band arrangement or two for Eddie Harvey's rehearsal band. Usually when I write arrangements I leave a lot to rehearsal and I don't dot every 'i' or cross every 't'. I never have. I'm a self-taught arranger and I still find it difficult to write everything down. If there's something I can't write, I rely on being able to explain it. But for this I knew I was going to a crowd of guys which included quite a lot of session men. So I really spent ages, for the

first time in my life, writing out the score, and double-check-
ing that I hadn't made any goofs in the copying . . . It sounded all right, so I gave myself a bit of encouragement big band
wise . . . In *Metropolis*, although I never studied musical
theory and know nothing about it, I did develop my own
theoretical approach to the way everything developed, the
overall texture, and the way different things were disentan-
gled from it. I was very pleased with that composition. I did
it a few times in England, and I did it abroad with the Danish
Radio Orchestra. That was another of those scenes where I
had to write these incredible arrangements for a band I'd
never even met before. I knew none of them and didn't even
speak the same language, and I had to go and do a radio
broadcast. I was terrified really. We did a gig in Finland with
the small band, then I went on to Denmark clutching these
arrangements — and it went very well. They had a line-up of
five trumpets and five trombones and so on. I couldn't resist
the opportunity to use these, and built up the arrangements
accordingly. Then when we came to record *Metropolis* I
decided to use the same size of band.

One of the reasons for the Arts Council's recent patronage of jazz was that Keith Winter, who began working
in the music department of the Arts Council in the late
'60s, knew a great deal about the jazz tradition, appreciated the quality of the British musicians he'd heard playing,
and felt that jazz should be as eligible for subsidies as any
of the other arts. Shortly after Graham Collier was awarded the very first grant to write his *Workpoints*, Westbrook
was given £500 to write his next work — *Metropolis*.
Two or three years of teaching every day and then burning
the midnight oil either writing or playing had utterly
exhausted him and he was ready for a change, a slower
pace:

I gave up teaching and moved out of London. I thought that
the 500 quid would tide me over because it seemed like a lot

The Mike Westbrook Concert Band, late 1960s, including Harry Miller (bass), Alan Jackson (drums), Westbrook (piano), and saxophones (*left to right*) Bernie Living (alto), Dave Chambers (tenor), Mike Osborne (alto), John Surman (soprano and baritone). Photo: Graham Keen.

of money to me, but of course, it was gone in a flash and I was really broke for a long time. I was heavily in the red for about three or four years really as a result of it!

But at least, for the first time, he had some breathing space — the time to think about what he was doing. And this is probably why *Metropolis* is for him the most musically satisfying piece he's done to date. It is certainly the most complex, and it features, among other things, a fairly extensive use of bi-tonality:

A lot of what I've done is very eclectic, I don't mind that, but I think I was into some kind of territory of my own with *Metropolis* — a kind of area which is very deep and spiritual and very musical. Although I called it *Metropolis*, it was no longer the *Marching Song* kind of thing where one had copious programme notes because it was illustrating things that were happening to people. *Metropolis* wasn't that kind of thing at all . . . it was a musical experience but, at the same time, related to impressions. Part of it was those kind of dawn breakfasts in motorway cafes and that strange sort of feeling at that time of day on the way back from gigs up north . . . going back to London on the motorway. Those were the sort of times that I'd be thinking about that composition, and all that went into it, and all the nostalgia for my roots . . . It was a very dense composition and had a lot of elements in it . . . I'd got into a kind of harmonic thing which was not the usual scales and modes, but two chords going simultaneously, more or less a sort of cluster . . . the composition came out of that . . . There were passages of arrangements that had different keys and things in it and all of it was related to sort of pedal sounds and needed to be held together in some way. I like rhythmic music. I always have. In fact, I like very funky rhythmic music. I'm not really into, and never have been, the sort of very-loose-time concept of playing. I tend to like it when it's straight ahead and pretty meaty. So the thing to do seemed to be to introduce a bass guitar and guitar into the group to take care of the basic business — and a second drummer. I wasn't thinking in terms of rock drumming particularly. It was just that these things were in 6/4 or 7/4 grooves and just needed a heavy rhythmic thing, and the conjunction of the two meant that we were playing, I suppose, jazz-rock really.

The first rehearsal of *Metropolis* was the scene of yet another of those confrontations Westbrook enjoys so much. He had asked Chris Spedding, who was beginning to make a name for himself on the rock circuits with a group called the Battered Ornaments, to play guitar with the band:

Chris came along to the rehearsal and that was very strange because . . . there was this entire band of jazz musicians, and then there was Chris Spedding with his amplifier and foot-pedals. Everybody was sussing him out very carefully . . . and, of course, he made it! By the end of the evening every-one was going up to him and saying "Hey, Chris!" Chris was very beautiful after the gig and said it had been a great experience, and that he'd never done anything like it and he'd love to do more! After that, when I had a ten-piece band I asked Chris to join it and he played with us for about a year . . . Things like *Metropolis* happen to you perhaps once or twice in a lifetime . . . The sort of thing where you set a seal on a whole range of experiences and bring them all together in one fusion. It was like a watershed, the top of one mountain, and there's a vista beyond it, and I think the next mountain is a long way away.

If *Metropolis* was Westbrook's ultimate musical statement of that period, *Earthrise* was probably his ultimate expression of the narrative/dramatic side of his conception. Bernard Miles had the idea of using the Mermaid Theatre as a venue for jazz, and he offered to commission a new work from Westbrook. The work was

Earthrise, and it marked the beginning of Westbrook's long and fruitful collaboration with John Fox who is deeply involved in experimental theatre. This association seems to be a very mutual affair:

> It's a very dynamic relationship. A lot of things have sprung from it. In the initial stages of a composition we sit and talk for hours, write letters . . . and it's like delving back into your whole life . . . we spend days going around London and the whole thing grows out of that. Then we produce our particular parts of it which in his case is mostly the theatre, and in mine is mostly the musical side.

Earthrise consisted of music played by a very big band, filmstrips, still photographs and visual effects projected onto a screen behind the band, and the dramatic use of lighting in the theatre. It would also have included dancing, acting and the use of costume and fancy-dress if the first performance hadn't been on a Sunday, which meant running up against the restrictive campaign of the Lord's Day Observance Society. But even confined to music, light-show, films and occasional props, *Earthrise* was a gargantuan event. Westbrook explains:

> It was like a piece of pure theatre really . . . I wrote a composition which was a narrative thing about the exploration of outer space really. It was a kind of light-hearted thing. The image rather appealed to me. It was like the great American frontier which used to be the Wild West. It began with a sort of cowboy song played by solo tenor, then we went into an old hoe-down type of thing and we suddenly go into orbit . . . I was imagining the astronauts creeping through space and listening to the radio messages from earth, and I thought you could probably have some kind of *Family Favourites* going on, messages to folks down there, and rather discreet music . . . Muzak sort of thing. So that got written in. Then they got nearer the moon and there was this feeling that once

they'd landed on it, then everything about the moon was going to change. It has always been this dream symbol, and when they get there and find that it's just a barren planet, pock-marked place, it's all going to change. So I did a whole thing, a sort of medley of moon songs — a terribly corny idea, but it seemed to amuse me at the time. We played *Blue Moon, Moonlight Serenade* where I attempted to ape the Glenn Miller arrangement, *Ol' Devil Moon*, then we went into a ballad . . . I needed a vocalist and Norma Winstone came into the band . . . The second half began with them arriving on the moon and it was a grotesque, nightmarish section. I used George Smith playing the tuba, and a young guy, an infant prodigy really, Mark Griffiths, who had this thing of sticking a microphone down the bassoon. So the second half began with George Khan playing electric saxophone and the tuba and all these deep, incredible instruments quite horrifying, and then resolving into heavy rock — utterly nightmarish! Then it went into a period of tension mirroring this thing of people just about to take this new step, this irrevocable step of landing on the moon . . . This resolved into a thing where they were all on the moon. Then the great idea was for everybody to go there and it would all be colonised and there would be a Hilton Hotel built there. And I thought there'd be the grand opening and they'd import all the session men from New York up there and they'd have one of those great big bands like the Thad Jones—Mel Lewis band. I wrote a tune called *Party Time* for that. This gave way to a rather reflective passage where the astronauts were round the other side of the moon which must be the loneliest place in the universe I should think — out of sight of earth and in total darkness. Then they return and there's the Earth and so the tune *Earthrise* which is like a hymn. As they get back to Earth there's this feeling that nothing has been changed by it all really . . . The critics who had all raved about *Metropolis* all said "What the hell is he doing now? The joke's gone too far!" There were the most indignant reviews in the press. From then on, my reputation plummeted even though I was really getting into something. "Senseless rock and roll riffs repeated ad nauseam," you know, people were just missing the point altogether. They even interpreted my deliberate use of known material as a lack of imagination or lack of originality, whereas my whole idea was to use and exploit those images which everybody would recognise. Of course, the audiences loved it, but the critics were very snide about it and thought I'd deserted the cause after *Metropolis* which they all thought was a great piece of far-out jazz. This really shook my faith in the critics!

Since *Earthrise*, Westbrook has collaborated regularly with John Fox in creating multi-media events, and this has involved such things as working with sword-swallowers, fire-eaters, high-divers, and various other circus-type acts. And also since *Earthrise* he has stuck to working with a small group, which included Norma Winstone for a year or so. Having a vocalist in the band encouraged Westbrook to start writing songs. His wife Caroline wrote the lyrics. This resulted in the *Love Songs* album which Westbrook calls 'a disappointment' and he explains why:

> It was a transition. I was getting out of a blowing jazz thing into a pop thing. It was difficult to get the natural, live feeling of the *Love Songs* band in the studio. Really we needed more production. It was a new thing. I didn't understand the use of the studio. I didn't understand double tracking. At that stage I didn't understand the best way to arrange that material for the recording because it was new material. The kind of chords involved were totally different from the dense things I'd been doing before. I really think with *Metropolis* I understood what I was doing, but with these things that were paradoxically much simpler, I was still tending to overload it. We weren't yet into that way of playing, even though Chris Spedding was in the band — if only

Mike Westbrook Band c.1970 *left to right*: Norma Winstone, John Warren, George Khan, Mike Osborne (hidden), Dave Holdsworth, Malcolm Griffiths, Paul Rutherford.

Chris himself had actually realised that he could have put me straight on a lot of things — also George Khan could have done so . . . at the time they realised what I was trying to do, and saw that it was a good thing, and a good direction, but it wasn't quite happening. It was only with the single, *Magic Garden*, recorded at the end of the session, and the next lot of songs, *Horizon*, that we really got it together. The *Love Songs* LP didn't do justice to the band or to the songs themselves.

Since then, Westbrook has gone much more deeply into pop — into the music and into the mystique of it. His music for Adrian Mitchell's *Tyger*, a musical about William Blake staged by the National Theatre in 1971, used a variety of pop styles. Solid Gold Cadillac is another phase of total commitment in Westbrook's programme of discovering things for himself:

> I think you find out by doing things . . . so I think one should do things and not be afraid of risking one's reputation or getting sullied in the process . . . I'm not closed to anything as a matter of principle . . . In fact I actually think I'm getting more and more open because I've found there can be much good in so many things. In fact, as a jazz musician, the way I was five years ago — I was incredibly stuck-up! . . . I'd scorned a lot of pop music . . . then I sat down and listened to the *Sergeant Pepper* LP one night and I was really turned on by it. Some really commercial music like Tamla Motown which is made to a formula, is *good* music, while some stuff which is arty and has the high-minded principles and everything . . . it's dire! There's got to be some other criteria and I don't know what it is! . . . Is *Puppy Love* good music or is it absolutely awful? Sometimes it's good, sometimes it isn't, and sometimes it's bloody pretentious! What interests me is the whole pop culture thing — from pop art onwards, and the kind of questions it's involved with. The thing in the musical press with Marc Bolan and David Bowie and so on is very much centred around this thing of what is showbiz? What is art? I don't think a lot of the jazz players have taken account of this. I think this is the core of the rift which may have developed in a way between me and the friends that have worked with me, even though I think many of them are still quite sympathetic. After *Metropolis*, which everybody could identify with, I think a lot of musicians too have felt that they couldn't go along . . . which is fair enough. But as far as I am concerned, I know that I want to ask those questions, and I think the arena in which those questions are being asked is pop . . . From going through a period when I couldn't bear to pick up the *Melody Maker*, I now read it every week because I think it's a fabulously interesting social thing. Among all the adulation and the bullshit, there's quite a lot of questioning going on. These things interest me too. Is it

possible for us to play *I Believe?* What difference does it
make? We now dress up on gigs. We've given ourselves a
new name because I'm fed up with being the Mike
Westbrook Band. I've had ten years of that and I feel that
it's not a true representation of a group which is a very even
thing between people . . . Alan Jackson and Malcolm
Griffiths have been working with me for ten years now,
George Khan for something like five years, and Phil Minton
is a long associate, and these are not just musical associations
— these people are more than friends. They are brothers
really . . . OK, we dress up and sometimes wear make-up
on stage. Does this invalidate what we do? Let people ask
and see. To me it seems quite logical, and in fact it's quite
fun and an enormous release to go into those things . . . I'm
less committed to some notion of musical purity or musical
development than to some kind of over-all concept. I can
see that with some musicians it would be wrong for them to
make that kind of bridge. Even to do anything that would
win over the listener by some form of presentation and so
on would be abhorrent to them . . . but I really enjoy it.
Not only the thing of getting a whole audience on their feet,
but I've played where there have been fire-eaters on stage,
children doing acrobatics, brass bands the lot! . . . What I'm
after is some kind of spiritual thing. This is a restless quest.
This feeling of terror before I do a thing is just the same
before *Marching Song* or *Release.* Nobody would believe
it listening to *Release*; it sounds so much fun. But one
approaches these things almost in a feeling of fear because
of what you're dabbling with, what you're playing with . . .
We're not just doing a bit of decoration around the fringes
of life for some jaded people. We're dealing with people's
emotions very deeply and we're part of a stream of
consciousness — even though a lot of the music we do is
throwaway stuff and quite good fun . . . I was reading a book
by Saul Bellow called *Dangling Man,* and you know where
he goes up to a party at his in-laws and finds this record

which he'd given to the daughter which she'd never played
— something like Handel or Mozart or something. He puts
it on and he realised that he was just an apprentice in human
suffering. That's what I feel sometimes about some other
music . . . we're all part of this thing and the sum total of
human existence is, in a way, suffering. We struggle to blot
it out, but the actual reality of humanity is suffering, and
some races and some people have come much more to
terms with it. In our world I don't think we have. We're very
shallow in a way . . . I feel very close to that . . . and I know
that this quality is there in all great art. There's one thing I
haven't mentioned, an odd thing which I did in the middle
of all this . . . as a result of my art studies, while I was doing
teacher training I spent a lot of time at the British Museum
and got very drawn to some Mayan sculptures. I spent a lot
of time just looking at these things and in a strange sort of
way I had a spiritual experience very much like the thing I'm
talking about — this enormous sadness. I was plunged into a
whole new spiritual vacuum by this experience . . . I had to
do something about it. I wanted to do some kind of composition. I had no idea what it was going to be because the idea
of writing music — notes — completely eluded me. I couldn't
think of it except in very broad terms. I eventually composed
something called *Copan Backing Track*. I latched on to the
mathematical aspects of their calendar which seemed to give
me some kind of structure to work on. There are three different cycles going on simultaneously which connect at different points. I wrote the composition for seven musicians
which seemed to be some kind of mystic number, and the
composition was seven hours long. It was entirely improvised with very carefully selected musicians, not people that
I work with regularly. It also involved a light show. It was like
a total cycle — a vigil sort of thing. It wasn't a performance as
such . . . I've never gone further out than I did with that thing
in a sense . . . I think I was really getting into something that
was terrifying really. I was terrified writing it and thinking

about it . . . really on edge, almost losing my mind really. It was very deep, very beautiful, very liberating . . . a kind of sacred thing almost. I haven't pursued it . . . it was probably a development of the *Metropolis* area. It was totally free, and yet not free in that it was structured, and the preparations, the discussions, the pre-recordings were part of some pattern, some sort of plan, and one was just some sort of instrument of this thing. We all wore overalls because we were just like technicians, people fulfilling some kind of function in a plan. It may take me years to resolve that thing.

Everything about Mike Westbrook seems to be more extreme than in most other musicians — the numerous false starts, the desperate early struggles, the praise, the blame, the size of his ventures, the length of his works, the totality of his commitment to whatever area he is working out. He has continually done the unexpected, and he has enlarged the consciousness, receptiveness, and potential of British musicians.

4

JOHN STEVENS
and TREVOR WATTS
The Spontaneous Music Ensemble

The Spontaneous Music Ensemble, which was formed by
John Stevens, Trevor Watts and Paul Rutherford in the
middle sixties and which has featured groups of all sizes
from big bands to duos, has been a major influence on the
British scene. If Mike Westbrook's main contribution has
been not to exclude areas, but to absorb multiple influences and fuse them into new syntheses, John Stevens has
made himself the virtual conscience and inspiration of a
whole school of players, by a severe process of questioning
and elimination.

Stevens and Watts have to be considered together
because they have been so closely associated over the
years. The music they make as a duo, Stevens on drums
and Watts on saxophones, has no predetermined themes
or melodies, no harmonies (obviously — because there is
no harmonic/chordal instrument), and no easily dis-
cernible regular rhythmic pulse. The resulting music is an
austere improvisation of percussive sounds — even Watts'
saxophone seems to function basically as a percussive
instrument — with occasional vocal interjections, moans
and wails from John Stevens. It is as if the internal skeleton
of jazz (regular pulse, fixed bar-lines and harmonies)
has been removed and replaced with the external skeleton

John Stevens at
the100 Club,
London, 1976
(photo © Jak
Kilby).

of an insect. The duo are not improvising on a structure:
The improvisation *is* the structure.

However posterity judges the intrinsic value of John
Stevens' music, his historical importance and his seminal
influence on the British scene are already established facts.

In the early 1960s he seemed to have everything going
for him as a hip member of the inner circle of London
musicians. He was the new drummer to watch. He
appeared regularly at the Ronnie Scott Club, and he was
much in demand with established musicians. Then suddenly, with the *volte-face* of a Saint Paul on the road to
Damascus, Stevens renounced the established scene,
turned down the more conventional work which was earning his bread and butter, and devoted himself entirely to
radical experiment in improvised music. His example

of total commitment (and that of Watts and Rutherford) was an act of faith which inspired many disciples and created, for the first time in this country, a solid avant-garde movement.

Before the SME took this stand, there had been individual attempts at radical experiment. But these were made by musicians who were still committed to playing conventional music, and did not give birth to an entirely self-contained and alternative way of playing. But some of the individuals had nevertheless achieved remarkable results. The late Joe Harriott, towards the end of the 1950s, had begun functioning almost schizophrenically with his quintet. In a two-hour concert he would play one hour of conventional music and one hour of experimental music,

and he even made LPs where conventional tracks alternated with profoundly experimental tracks, or where one whole side was conventional and the other side experimental. Harriott was one of the very first mature jazz musicians to become a self-conscious experimenter, and with the help of his sidemen, trumpeter Shake Keane, pianist Pat Smythe, bassist Coleridge Goode, and either Phil Seamen or Bobby Orr on the drums, he created a rich new musical language, and a way of playing which owed little or

Michael Garrick (piano), Joe Harriott, Tony Coe, Ian Carr (photo courtesy M. Garrick).

nothing to his American counterpart, Ornette Coleman. The Harriott Quintet shook the inherent conservatism of the British scene in the late '50s and early '60s, but because it still had one foot in conventional music, and also perhaps because it was ahead of its time, it has not produced a school of disciples or imitators.

On the other hand, the commitment that characterises SME has been almost religious in its intensity, and it has clear political overtones. Here, obviously, is an alternative to the factory-belt consumer society, and here, certainly, is a music whose deepest impulse is not to make money, but to express the personal vision of the musicians. During the sixties, it was the 'still, small, voice' of sanity in a world apparently going mad and rushing like Gadarene swine into the vortex of 'Swinging London'. The breadth of the SME's appeal was intoxicating to musicians whose prime impulse was to look for new ways of expression, and it was also attractive to musicians who were still involved in more conventional music but wanted to expand their playing conception. The character of John Stevens has some relevance here. Because he had a very generous temperament and was utterly without malice, although he had strong convictions about the kind of music he wanted to produce, he was not in the least prejudiced about the kind of musicians he wanted to work with. So the SME became, over the years, a sort of open house for any musicians who wanted to explore the group's concept of playing. As a result, almost every contemporary jazz musician of note in London has played with it at one time or another, and has had his mental horizons expanded by the experience.

What influences and experiences combined to create John Stevens' musical vision and endow him with so much conviction? And what formative influences does he have in common with Trevor Watts?

Trevor Watts
with Harry
Miller,
Amsterdam,
1978 (photo ©
Jak Kilby).

They met in the RAF in 1958 when they'd both, inde-
pendently, signed on for five years in order to be able to
join the military band and learn their instruments. During
the 1950s several would-be jazz musicians adopted this
curious method of studying music because there was simply nowhere else where a jazz musician could get organised
study and practice time. Also in the RAF band at the same
time as Watts and Stevens, and for the same reasons, were
the trombonist Paul Rutherford, later to be one of the leading members of the avant-garde, saxophonist Bob Downes
who was later to create his 'Open Music', and the drummer John Spooner who was to become a member of the
John Dankworth band in the late 1960s. They spent some

time studying at the RAF school of music at Uxbridge, then Stevens, Rutherford and Watts were posted to Germany.

There's no doubt that the three and a half years they spent in Germany had a crucial effect on their later development. First of all, they were able to spend a great deal of time playing together; and then they were able to take advantage of the kind of musical experiences Germany offered. The arts in general are treated with much more respect in Germany than they are in England. There is more open-mindedness, more adventure, and more sheer interest in things artistic and more concern with all types of contemporary music. Furthermore, a strong cultural lead is given by the media – in particular the radio stations and television networks. Trevor Watts gives more details:

> The German radio made us very much aware of the new developments in jazz . . . we had the opportunity to hear the new things almost as soon as they were recorded. And on the radio they didn't just play one track of an album, they'd play the whole side of, say, a record like *Chasin' the Trane* . . . I remember hearing Ornette Coleman's *Tomorrow Is the Question* there . . . I taped it and I kept playing it. There was something really appealing about it and I couldn't understand what it was at the time. I just didn't have a clue! . . . Then there was a concert at Cologne with Miles Davis and Coltrane – Miles playing that green lacquered trumpet! . . . And the Charlie Mingus group came over with Eric Dolphy – all sorts of groups that you couldn't get in England at that particular time . . . So even then we were starting to try and play freer things . . . and because you were used to hearing new things, it just felt like a natural development from Charlie Parker.

There was also a jazz bar in Cologne where there was something happening just about every night of the week, and Stevens was able to sit-in there with various

Americans, the British alto saxophonist the late Derek Humble, and German musicians such as Manfred Schoof and Alex Von Schlippenbach — both of whom were to become internationally famous in the 1960s. Stevens, Watts and Rutherford also ran their own cellar jazz club where Derek Humble sat in regularly. After this baptism of fire, returning to London was something of a cultural damp squib. John Stevens describes the shock he experienced:

> Coming back to London, I found it strange . . . one of the first things I heard was a jazz programme on BBC radio, and they played a tiny section from the middle of a John Coltrane record, it might have been something like *Impressions* or *Chasin' the Trane*, and the disc-jockey said: "What on earth's happened to John Coltrane? Listen to this!" It was as if he'd thought Coltrane had gone crazy. And I found this amazing, because if you'd been really following Coltrane you could see the logical development of what he was trying to do.

There was also, predictably, disappointment and disillusionment when Stevens began working as a professional drummer on the London scene. Again, his character, as well as the state of the scene, has a great deal of relevance here, because Stevens seems to be one of those rare people who are not corrupted by the process of growing up — who in fact are hardly capable of the usual compromises and adjustments that most people try to make in order to fit in to some recognised social role. Somehow, he seems to have maintained an almost childlike innocence and purity of vision which, time after time, has come up against actuality with a hard jolt. Pain is felt, evasive action is taken, but the innocence remains. This pattern of experience seems to have continued to occur ever since his adolescence:

At first, I envisaged being a tap-dancer . . . my dad was involved in that, and I used to go and see musical films featuring Ginger Rogers and Fred Astaire . . . Other than that, my main hobby as a kid was painting and drawing, which lasted right up until I went to art school. As soon as I started to be taught or organised, it conflicted with the way I felt . . . So I didn't actually start playing music until after the disillusion with painting and drawing set in. That would be when I was about seventeen. I started playing on a biscuit tin while listening to records . . . After leaving art school I started work in a commercial art studio which really pissed me off . . . I couldn't relate pure painting with this commercial thing which I'd never really thought about until I suddenly had to make a living . . . I was given the bullet because I just reacted against it so much . . . Then I realised that I just wanted to play music . . . The thing that appealed to me about music was that it was a collective experience and expression.

It was probably the collective strength of the musical experience which helped them all to weather the harsh external discipline of military life for five years. But even so, a powerful anti-military feeling and resistance to authority grew up in the band. As Stevens says: "When you get so many guys all united in wanting the same things, there's not so much that authority can do." So they had things pretty much their own way and even ran regular big band sessions in the NAAFI.

When he came to London in 1963 he was searching for the same kind of collective identity which he had experienced in the RAF, but once more business got in the way of pleasure and fulfilment:

When I came to London and started playing professionally as a jazz musician, I found that you had to play with people in a very cool way, and you had to get used to being told: "Oh, could you play this way? You know, ding-dingadingchoc." Either I misunderstood jazz, or jazz wasn't being played in the right way. The feeling I got initially attracted to in jazz was its feeling of total freedom of self-expression . . . but some people as soloists just wanted a clear way — a time-keeping drummer — they didn't want to converse with the drums, or they didn't want the drums to interfere with their monologue or their particular statement . . . I thought the thing to do would be to play at Ronnie Scott's Club, because that's where I'd heard a lot of jazz. But the more I came in contact with the profession, the more it began to feel like the world of commercial art which I'd disliked so much . . . I needed a group involvement which I didn't have on the professional jazz scene. There were occasions when you would have that, when people were just getting together for the sheer joy of playing together. But I found it less and less in the actual gigs, and more and more in the afternoon rehearsals and the things I was doing in my spare time . . . So a significant thing was finding the Little Theatre Club. You got in there with people who were interested in the same group experience and the music was allowed to develop day by day, literally.

Trevor Watts came to live in London in 1963. At first he played with the New Jazz Orchestra, which also included his old RAF associate Paul Rutherford in the trombone section. The two of them spent a lot of time playing together, writing and working out new approaches to the music, and it was almost inevitable that they would sooner or later reunite with John Stevens, because they too were not finding the kind of fulfilment they expected in London. Sure enough, Stevens and Watts bumped into each other quite accidentally, and began to play together again. Then a friend of John Stevens discovered the Little Theatre Club, and the lady who runs it, Jean Pritchard, allowed him to use the club six nights a week — regardless of attendance or profit — from eight o'clock in the evening until eleven and occasionally to one o'clock. Trevor Watts says of her: "She's fantastic, because it doesn't draw all that many people and she lets us use it! . . . She must be an angel or something!" And it is a sobering thought that the development, even the continuation, of jazz in Britain has often relied on the chance generosity of a few remarkable individuals.

Having the use of club premises six nights a week immediately changed the climate of the British scene, because John Stevens, with typical generosity, offered evenings there to any musicians who had nowhere else to play. When the club began functioning for the first time on January 3rd 1966, the rising generation of jazz musicians came into the open and showed their colours. Only a few months previously, Stevens had made another major breakthrough when he'd persuaded Bryant Marriott, the BBC *Jazz Club* producer, to broadcast some of these new musicians in their own right for the first time. He'd told Marriott of the large number of underground, unheard musicians with powerful and diverse talents: there was the Chris McGregor Band, there was the whole team who lived at 80 Sinclair Road — Mike Pyne, Chris Pyne, Ron Matthewson, Ray Warleigh — and visitors to that address such as Kenny Wheeler and Alan Skidmore. Then there were Trevor Watts, Paul Rutherford, Pete Lemer, Jeff Clyne, the Mike Taylor Trio, Henry Lowther and the Group Sounds Five. Stevens had been dreaming naïvely, as he later admits, of a huge broadcast featuring several groups and terminating in a massive freely improvised finale involving everybody. It didn't turn out like that. The broadcast was in fact done by the John Stevens Septet (Kenny Wheeler, Alan Skidmore, Ray Warleigh, Chris Pyne, Mike Pyne, Ron Matthewson and Stevens), and the Group Sounds Five. It was an immensely successful broadcast, and a crucially important one because it created a precedent. From then on, for five years or so, the bands for BBC *Jazz Club* were drawn as much from the new generation as from the older ones.

The Little Theatre Club rapidly established itself as the platform and crucible for the ideas and experiments of the rising generation of musicians. Apart from providing a regular weekly playing spot for numerous little-known musicians and groups, it also became the place where all kinds of musicians known and unknown dropped in to listen or to sit-in when there was a loosely organised blowing session — which happened most nights. When the Ronnie Scott Club moved to new premises in Frith Street, and the Old Place became vacant, the centre of gravity of the scene shifted. John Stevens explains what happened:

> A thing like the Little Theatre Club succeeds when the musicians stick together and carry on. It wasn't initially a political movement, but it became that — it was anti the establishment which was, of course, the Ronnie Scott Club. One day I was asked to go over and see Ronnie Scott and he asked me if I would give up the Theatre Club and run the Old Place using the same sort of policy as we'd had at the Theatre Club. He made this offer because if nothing was going on at the premises the landlord or something would take possession of the property, and the Scott Club wanted to keep hold of it so that it could be turned into a Chinese gambling club. Ronnie said to me: "I don't know how long it'll be — it could be two weeks or six months. That's the chance you'll have to take" . . . I refused to take it on because we had a place which might go on for ever and it felt strong to me. We might not get many people in the audience up there and in any case it wasn't very big, but it offered a kind of freedom to develop your music. Anyway, I said I wouldn't do it, and the funny thing was that two weeks later it was, "Good old Ronnie! — Opening the first club for young musicians and really

encouraging them!" There was a list of people who would be playing there, and my name was on it!

Trevor Watts fills out the picture:

What happened eventually, was that all the bands who were playing for the Theatre Club drifted away and moved to the Old Place because you were paid £3 a night there, and it was more prestigious. And people would say to us, "Why have you quit the scene? Why have you stayed on your own?" But what had happened was that we'd stayed in the same place, and everybody else had moved. Eventually the Old Place did close down . . . but the Theatre Club is still going now in 1972!

In fact, the only band which remained at the Theatre Club was the SME which, at that time, comprised Derek Bailey, Evan Parker, Paul Rutherford, Trevor Watts, Barry Guy, Kenny Wheeler and John Stevens, though other musicians, in particular the bass players Jeff Clyne, John Ryan and Bruce Cale, were also involved with the group from time to time. From the moment he started running the Theatre Club, Stevens' life became much harder. He was playing there, and organising the presentation of other bands six nights a week, but the average wage he could expect was no more than a few shillings a night. He had to work during the day as a packer, and he economised on rent by living in a caretaker flat. The rent was nominal, but he had to keep the premises clean and look after them generally, which was another drain on the energies. His wife also worked part-time. For a few months Stevens, Watts and Evan Parker went to live in Denmark where there is more of an audience for experimental music, but they couldn't get work permits and had to leave. Before returning to England, Stevens spent some time in Amsterdam playing with saxophonist John Tchicai. There's no doubt that this period abroad, associating with

Continental and American musicians, helped Stevens to clarify his own ideas.

It could be said that John Stevens has been carrying on a kind of guerrilla warfare against conventional musical thinking and, although he would not put it so forcefully himself, there is a degree of revolutionary fervour in his approach to musical experiment or 'finding new ways of doing things'. The musical vision of SME has grown out of this natural exploration by the band of alternative directions. The whole idea that the rhythm section should beat out its regular pulse and the horns should play solos over this pulse is questioned. Instead, each instrument in a group is given an equally important part to play. In other words the instruments of the rhythm section are playing an equally important part in the improvisation as the so-called melodic instruments. Trevor Watts describes what happens next:

> The difference between SME and other groups is in the second stage of development. The first stage was that the rhythm section learned from the horns. All played equally together but still in a linear way. The second stage, which we are in, means that the horns have to learn from the drum and from the relationship between bass and drum, in particular the conversational qualities of playing moment by moment together. This means that rhythm becomes the key factor. The role of the note is therefore diminished, and, obviously, if you're relating to the bass on equal terms, the acoustics of the music are greatly affected.

This leads on naturally to a further step. If all instruments are functioning rhythmically and melodically there is no need for a 'rhythm section' to function as a unit any more. The traditional instrumentation of a jazz group is therefore redundant so far as these purposes and intentions are concerned. The music can be made equally well

with any combination of instruments. So they began functioning with duos and trios (drums and one or two saxophones) as well as with larger units. When John Stevens
returned from the Continent the SME was a trio with
Stevens on drums and the two saxophonists Trevor Watts
and Evan Parker. It was at this point that Trevor could not
identify with the conception. He explains:

> . . . John felt a really strong thing about a way of playing
> which nobody understood . . . There was a certain thing he
> wanted, a group music, a relationship that I obviously wasn't
> hearing at that time. In the middle of a gig we were doing I
> quit the band and the SME was down to a duo with Evan
> and John . . . But I'm glad that I left at the time because I
> learned from the split — I learned that what I wanted to do
> was to play with that band . . . It's still the same direction for
> John . . . and I've learned the language now . . .

In the soul-searching period when he was away from
SME, Watts formed a group with Paul Rutherford, Barry
Guy and sometimes Derek Bailey. They called themselves
Amalgam and Watts describes their music as "a group
music that was more to do with 'sounds' and changing
textures than anything else". Before too long he was back
with John Stevens, not that the period with Amalgam was
unproductive. As he puts it:

> The area we were covering was new territory also, except I
> found John's method eventually more attractive.

He goes on to describe their current work:

> The music that John and I play now is purely rhythmic real-
> ly and the sound is not important in the least, except that if
> you listen to it from that point of view it's quite interesting
> also. But the whole point of the music is to get beyond the
> sound of it into the content of it, which requires a different
> way of listening . . . The stress is on playing together. It's
> getting stronger now than it ever has been . . . You're not

paraphrasing each other which is of course what used to happen in an earlier form of the music . . . When it's at its best I'm hearing wholly what John's doing and yet I'm playing what I want to play at the same time relating to that rhythm. That's the strength — it's two people standing there on completely equal terms . . . and the most important thing is the listening process, not what you're actually playing yourself. The best results happen, for example, when I don't get involved in what I'm playing myself at all . . . I'm just a huge pair of ears. A giant ear is what I want to be. Through this discipline, I've found that even if I'm playing with a ten-piece group, I can hear all the things that are happening and know where my position is in that. John has evolved a lot of exercises and things to help arrive at this kind of awareness. That's what he's doing in his workshops.

Paul Rutherford
London, 1972
(photo © Jak
Kilby).

The music of the SME is now almost completely improvised and there is no predetermined composition as such, but obviously, when people have been playing together for years they develop an understanding and an empathy which enables them to create their musical forms spontaneously. The whole development of the SME has been a gradual movement away from predetermined structures. When they first started, they used written themes or thematic fragments, and once these were played, the improvisations were developments of the melodic motifs. They had, from the outset, abandoned harmonic improvisation. Also, in the early days, there would be solos as well as group improvisation, and these were primarily melodic as opposed to rhythmic variations on the themes. Later on, the predetermined passages would include 'head' arrangements as well as, or instead of, written fragments — in other words they would talk the structure through. John Stevens still uses this method in his workshops.

The SME does very occasionally play concerts at festivals or colleges in provincial British towns. It also, perhaps even more rarely, plays abroad — usually on the Continent. So how are John Stevens and Trevor Watts managing to survive — and, even more remarkably, maintain their enthusiasm and impetus? Trevor Watts manages to make enough money to live by doing proof-reading for a publisher, and his wife is a music copyist. Stevens has no ready-made channel for obtaining money, but, in his usual way, manages to turn this disadvantage to spiritual and social use:

> Through the music and this sort of group thing which forces a very close relationship with your associates, and where you actually go through all the conflicts and tensions in a very close personal way, it's led to me working in youth clubs and things like that . . . I see kids I'm working with that are at

such a tangent with what's going on, don't know which way to go, have got bad home lives, kids between fourteen and twenty — they haven't got a direction and the music scene, which is a very dominant factor in our lives, doesn't help in any way because, in the main, the music they come in contact with is created for business reasons and the image of it is there and can be changed according to how the fashion goes . . . What I'm seeing is these kids taking handfuls of Mandrax and later getting on to heroin and dying . . . It was pretty unusual when we were fifteen or sixteen to hear of a kid who'd killed himself by an overdose of drugs or by accidentally drinking too much, but most of these kids today know kids in their block or the flats across the road who have died through overdoses of drugs etc . . . So I work twice a week at a youth club as an assistant youth leader, I've also got a jazz workshop on Mondays at Ealing Music School. I get paid for the Ealing thing £6.50, and I get £2.50 per night at the youth club. Those three things on their own are quite demanding because they involve helping people to get involved in a group situation. I've also started teaching drumming now at the youth club . . . Another thing I do is to run the Theatre Club and play there. On average when I play there I guess I would get 50p for it which doesn't really cover the fare. On top of that, I rehearse a couple of times a week and I'm obviously on the lookout for gigs. I think of myself as a musician, somebody who's working at becoming a better musician, and, obviously, I hope to get work with the SME. I do occasionally get some money from the Performing Rights Society but not much because we don't get very many engagements. And I occasionally get something from the sales of our LPs — but again not much. So I draw supplementary benefit in order to help me carry on as a musician. Say I didn't get supplementary benefit, then I would have to give up the youth club, the workshop, and the Theatre Club which aren't nearly lucrative enough to live on, and take a full-time day job if I could get one — and if I did, it might bring me in nearly £20 a week if I was lucky, because I haven't got any particular skill . . . I've done a nine to five job before, and so has Trevor . . . and I know it would cut down considerably on my involvement with music and the social work I do through the music . . . The tensions come from this situation . . . I mean I've got a wife and two children in a flat which is not as expensive as most flats, but it's expensive for me . . . I'm scared of not having any money. I'm scared of being so on the edge that I'm going to run into a period where I haven't money. Maybe they'll get fed up with giving me supplementary benefit and then I'll have to get that day job. And that would be a trap because I'd have to spend all those hours to get only a little bit of money every week which takes away my possibilities of getting on with the music or finding musical work . . . I know my own limitations as musician. Trevor and I are working very hard. We rehearse as much as we can . . . And we're working at something that we can't do very well — relating to the achievements of people you've respected over the years, say, like Max Roach. When I think of the way he plays and how much he's given to the music, I accept our situation as far as I can. I do feel that I deserve more work than I get, probably . . . I'm not comparing the SME with Charlie Parker or anything, but it has been through a hell of a lot of changes equivalent to the people playing with it. We fail in a way because most people won't know what we sound like today and because of this we get little work. What I would like is for people to get familiar with change because I see change as the only constant. If people got familiar with change which is the constant thing, say, about the way Trevor and I and anyone else are involved in our music, then there might be more interest in what we are doing . . . Anyway if people become more familiar with change, then automatically they become more tolerant as people.

5

JON HISEMAN

Unlike many other British jazz musicians, Jon Hiseman had no real false starts. From an early age he knew he wanted to play the drums and with typical single-mindedness and determination he set about doing just that. He was spared even the usual incomprehension and opposition from his family:

> It seemed that there was no conflict between a normal sub-urban upbringing which I had and just simply being a musician. There'd been lots of musicians in my family, so there was never any sort of terrible problem about my doing it.

By 1966 Hiseman was still a semi-professional (he earned his living at a non-musical day-job), but he'd already established himself as one of the most promising and respected young drummers on the jazz scene. Apart from being the drummer with Group Sounds Five, a quintet led by trumpeter/violinist Henry Lowther and including such people as Lyn Dobson (tenor sax), Ron Rubin or Jack Bruce (bass), and Tony Hyams or Ken McCarthy (piano), Hiseman had also played on the first LPs made by the new generation of musicians: *Western Reunion* by the New Jazz Orchestra, and *Pendulum* by the Mike Taylor Quartet. Talking of this period, Hiseman says:

> I had to get up at 8 a.m. and go to work all day. I'd get home at about 6 p.m., have something to eat and then practise till

about 8 p.m., then go out to play a gig or rehearse. I'd be going to bed after 1 a.m. Then the next day the whole process would repeat itself . . . The problem was that Group Sounds Five would rehearse three nights a week but only do one actual gig a month . . . And the Mike Taylor Quartet — those albums were made as a result of Mike Taylor, Tony Reeves, Dave Tomlin and myself meeting in a film studio at Ilford twice a week for six months — and that was an hour's drive away from my home!

The frustrations of this way of life are obvious. Apart from the schizophrenic exhaustion of doing two jobs, living two lives, there was also the nagging awareness that he was totally committed to neither, and Jon Hiseman doesn't like doing things by halves. Crisis point came in 1966 when he realised that to develop any further as a drummer and musician he would have to become a professional and earn his living by playing. The snag was that there wasn't enough work in Britain to keep a regular jazz group employed, and for Hiseman this was perhaps the biggest drawback of the British scene:

One of the things that struck me very early on was that the finest music had come out of regular units . . . I never heard good records from a pick-up group. I heard groups like Ellington's big band and Coltrane's magnificent band on record after record, developing and changing as they fought out new areas as a unit, an identifiable unit. I could identify with each one of the people as a young fan and see their development. This seemed to me to be crucial to the life of the music.

But he saw possibilities for this kind of continuity and development on the rock scene where economics enabled groups to stay together as identifiable units. Also on that scene, Hiseman saw possibilities of achieving the one thing he craved most of all — to play the drums all day and every

Jon Hiseman, c.1970

day. With characteristic clearsightedness — and ruthlessness — he describes the dilemma that confronted him and
the steps he took to solve it:

> I quit the jazz scene not because I didn't like jazz, but
> because the only way for me to get good was to play six
> nights a week. I heard these guys who'd come up in the old
> school and who'd been playing for twenty years six nights a
> week, playing like gods, like dreams, and I knew I could do
> it given six nights a week for ten years, because, for me,
> you've got to sit down at your instrument and it's got to be
> the most comfortable place on earth. If that isn't like home,
> then you can forget it . . . and obviously it wasn't home if you
> were playing as little as I was . . . Also, I'd always felt that my
> instrument was grossly overpowering the way I wanted to
> play it when compared with a double bass or piano. The way
> I wanted to play drums, it was like a symphony orchestra
> instead of having three percussion and forty violins, having

forty percussion and three violins. The symphony orchestra is self-balancing because they didn't have amplification when the format was gradually built up, but the piano, bass, drum thing, the way I was developing was a grossly unbalanced thing. The chance of being able to play unrestricted by problems of volume was too good to be missed. Most of the great small group drummers had come up through the big bands. The big bands had taught them control at low volume as a result of having had years of really being able to play the thing and develop their muscles, because you need to be able to play very loudly in order to play quietly. The control that enables you to play *pianissimo* but very thickly comes as a result of really having had a good hammer for several years . . . So it's a very complicated thing, and basically, I wouldn't say that it was a strictly musical thing. In other words, I didn't say, "Jazz is dreadful, jazz is rubbish! I don't want to know about improvising, I just want to play pop music, I want to make money and everything." It was nothing to do with that. It was a much more complex thing to do with drums as drums and also to do with what I'd grown up to expect and what I was left with.

Ironically, just at the time when Hiseman was desperately impatient to turn fully professional, he refused several offers from leaders of established jazz groups:

In the end I became everyone's favourite deputy, and several jazz leaders came to me and said, "You know, so-and-so's leaving, the guy you've been depping for. Would you like to join me?" Each time I really wanted to do it, and I'd say, "What are you doing?" and they'd say, "Well, we've got another gig in two weeks' time, and then we're not doing anything for six weeks, and then we've got another gig. Then we've got a tour — four days — should be able to pay you £12 for the four days". . . And I began to see that I wouldn't be able to even afford to run the car that I was using to carry my drums about!

Eventually, Jon Hiseman accepted an offer to join Graham Bond's band, threw in his day job and was at last a full-time professional. And how could Graham Bond afford to employ Jon? Graham had burst on to the jazz scene, apparently out of nowhere, in about 1960 when he joined the Don Rendell Quintet. He was a virtuoso alto sax player and soon made a reputation as an aggressively avant-garde musician. That quintet made an LP called *Roarin'* which received high praise and a three-star rating in *Downbeat*. This was one of the first British LPs to get such a good review, and it was a unique breakthrough — an invasion of exclusively American territory, and the first evidence of the USA's acceptance of British equality in the noble art of jazz. Until then, we'd always been, like British heavyweights, good or not-so-good losers. Certain individuals had, of course, made some impact on the American scene, but this was the first time that an entirely homegrown product, an LP made in Britain by a British band, had been totally and unequivocally accepted on the other side of the Atlantic. A marked improvement in the group's work situation might reasonably have been expected, but in fact it made little noticeable difference to their economic viability. Then in 1962 Graham stepped out of the jazz scene and concentrated on playing the piano or organ and singing the blues, and spicing the mixture with some alto solos. Four years later Jon Hiseman joined him on drums and analyses the situation as follows:

> Graham was a crusader, a path-finder. He was playing music with an improvisatory element in it, an element which we take for granted in jazz but which, of course, had never existed in pop music. And the blues was the public's link between improvised music and pop music. In other words, a chord sequence like a thirty-two bar standard chord sequence doesn't repeat quickly enough and it's too

complex in its movements generally for an audience to identify with the chord sequence, so they identify with the
melody. Any attempt to improvise, not on the melody
(which trad bands did), but on the chord sequence, which is
what modern jazz (if we must use these terms) was doing,
lost the audience, which is why jazz was never as popular as
ballads or pop music where the melody is sung. What blues
did was to provide a sequence which was so simple that, no
matter what was being played over it, the audience knew
exactly where it was, and the cycle was always completed as
you got to the resolution and back to the tonic. So the blues
became the bridge between pop music which was based on
melody and a music which was based on something so
strong that it was like melody – the blues sequence over
which you could improvise as freely as you liked. So the
bridge between improvised music and pop music was the
blues as I see it. Graham Bond was one of the pioneers of
that. Without him there wouldn't have been what we've got
today – bands like Yes and Cream and Hendrix and all that.
They couldn't have come into existence without the way
being laid by people like Graham Bond and John Mayall. I
was very proud to be a member of both of those bands during their most path-finding periods, when things were just
beginning to turn, when just a little push over the edge and
they could have made it.

It was probably from John Mayall that Hiseman learnt the
importance of style – not so much in the actual music, but
in the way the music was presented. Mayall had a deep
knowledge of, and love for, the blues, and his singing
sounded amazingly authentic. In the early 1960s only a
handful of British singers could sing a convincing blues –
Long John Baldry, Eric Burdon, Mick Jagger were
perhaps the only others who could compare with Mayall in
their mastery of the idiom. But it was Mayall's 'style', the
way he projected his image and his personality, rather than

his blues artistry, which rescued him from the salary of a commercial artist in the Manchester area and established him at the end of the 1960s as a dollar millionaire in the United States. It was during that decade that the Western world began to become aware of the economic value of narcissism: look long enough and hard enough in the mirror and you may begin to see yourself as you appear to others. It is only a short step from there to actually setting about creating what you see.

John Mayall has always been one of nature's originals and has never been shy. ("You want to know me? Then read my diary!" He was an obsessive diarist.) He eventually settled for the leathery, weather-beaten image of a hero of a spaghetti western, and, on sunny days, travelling up the M1 to various gigs, he would have himself tied in the supine position on the roof-rack of the band vehicle. This meant that he could go onstage with his shirt wide open and display a deeply bronzed chest to the audience. The fact that his back was white as a fungus didn't trouble him at all. He knew the great secret: what you seem to be is much more important than what you actually are.

He was also totally matter-of-fact in the way he set about projecting his image to the public. Sitting in the bandroom with his group before playing, he would suddenly break off the easy conversation and stand up saying: "Time for a pose!" Then, after seeing that all his gear was carefully in place — suede shirts or jackets, big leather belts, and a stetson on his head — he would stride into the auditorium and strike statuesque poses staring poker-faced into the eyes of anyone who cared or dared to meet his gaze. To idiot questions from adoring fans he would bark laconic and enigmatic replies. Back in the privacy of the bandroom he would recount to his musicians what he'd done, said, and seen, for their amusement. And this fastidious separation of the private and public self certainly worked . . . and kept him working.

Although Graham Bond and, more particularly perhaps, John Mayall were the great popularisers of the blues and improvised music, there was an *éminence grise* behind them . . . Alexis Korner, the father of British blues and the man who paved the way for the whole phenomenon. He began functioning in the 1950s, and both aspects of the later Bond–Mayall syndrome, the improvisation and the image projection, were given their fullest expression in Alexis' Blues Incorporated. Improvisation has been so germane to Alexis' conception that at one time or another practically every British jazz musician has played with his band. To this extent he initiated the first moves in breaking down the artificial barriers between jazz and other forms of music. At various times his band included such people as Ginger Baker and Phil Seamen, Graham Bond,

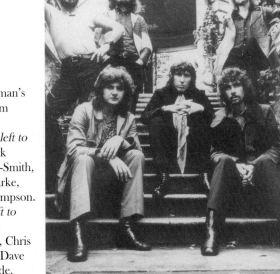

Jon Hiseman's Colosseum c.1970.
Standing left to right: Dick Heckstall-Smith, Mark Clarke, Dave Clempson.
Sitting left to right: Jon Hiseman, Chris Farlowe, Dave Greenslade.

Jack Bruce, Mick Jagger, and also virtuoso soloists such as
Kenny Wheeler and Ray Warleigh.

And Alexis Korner's image-projection, his separation of
the private and public self, was even more extreme than
Mayall's. In private, Alexis is an extremely sensitive and
sophisticated individual, his voice a furry drawl with an
accent which would grace the Officers' Mess of any
Guards' regiment. But in public performance he presents
the tough, flashy image of the American West — the high
boots, leather and snakeskin clothes, wide belts, wide-
brimmed hats, and the virile cigar jutting from a long,
hawk-like face. And even the purring, Rolls-Royce voice
undergoes an amazing transformation, losing its urbanity
and barking out barbaric interpretations of the blues. But
Alexis was ahead of his time and never seemed to get the
backing and support of a large publicity machine, so he
didn't achieve the vast audiences of a super-star . . . and
perhaps he didn't want this anyway. Time after time when
he seemed to be on the point of financial canonisation, he
simply changed tack and began exploring new areas . . .
always the prophet, never the Pope.

When Jon Hiseman left the Mayall band in the later
1960s, he found himself once more at the crossroads:

> I couldn't go back to playing jazz. I'd got use to a way of life,
> touring, a big-time way of life if you like where you play to
> large audiences. I couldn't really face going back to playing
> in dreadful pubs to forty people and doing a day-job as well,
> which is what it would have meant. I couldn't have stood
> doing sessions. That would have driven me round the bend.
> So that was out for me, and that's where a lot of the musi-
> cians who do play jazz now make up their money. So I knew
> that I had to form a band because there was nobody else for
> me to go and play with at the time . . . To a certain extent
> I've always been a crusader in that I've always played music
> that I've considered wasn't commercial. I've always tried to

educate if you like. It's a terribly pompous thing to say I
know, but it's not enough to go out there and give people
what they want. You have to try and open new doors for
them too, particularly when you're in a situation where you
know so much more about what you're doing than the listener does. You have to communicate on two levels, one at a
level that they can understand and another at a much more
edifying level, in order for your music to be able to progress.
If we stayed at the level of the mass all the time, music would
still be at the level of Bing Crosby and Bob Hope . . . So I
tried to form a band which was an improvisatory group, but
I tried to be very clever about the material we used so that I
could reach people on two separate levels. I was also working on another theory which is that it's not what you do but
the way you do it that matters to an audience. This takes me
back to one of my basic premises about jazz which is that in
the 1940s, when the big bands were in vogue they were really playing a division of pop music. It was the pop music of
the era and people danced to it . . . it seemed to me that you
could put anything across if you did it in an entertaining way.
So I formed Colosseum to do all the things that a rock group
does, but to play music that was as complex as anything that
anybody was playing. And I proved to my own satisfaction
that it could be done.

Hiseman's crusading reached a climax in 1970 when
Colosseum became the rhythm section for his earlier love,
the New Jazz Orchestra, and played a concert at the
Lanchester Arts Festival. By that time Colosseum's reputation was at its peak, and the concert hall was packed with
about two thousand rock fans, who listened in wrapt
silence to the orchestra and gave it a standing ovation at the
end of the set. And, as Jon Hiseman points out:

That so-called 'idiot' audience didn't clap and rave like
pub audiences do — at the loudest, fastest number. The
piece that got the best ovation was an arrangement by the

late Mike Taylor of Segovia's composition *Study*, which featured a sensitive duet by Henry Lowther and Barbara Thompson . . . We did a series of concerts all over England with that band and things that pleased musicians most also went down best with audiences — in other words, the musical values of musicians and audiences actually coincided! I don't believe this business of audiences not knowing — they do know, but, you see, people are not putting their music across properly. The biggest success Colosseum had as a live number was Mike Gibbs' *Tanglewood 63*. The time signatures on that are mind-bending, yet I've got a record of that piece with the whole audience clapping along with it!

About a year later (in 1971), Colosseum disbanded, probably because it had achieved all that it could, and perhaps its major achievements were twofold: first, it had been able to persuade businessmen to invest in a music which was largely instrumental and which featured improvisation; second, it had created a large audience for that kind of music. But the audience wasn't quite large enough as Hiseman points out:

Unfortunately, it cost £12,000 more than we earned to keep that band on the road, so whilst the record companies paid that money, somebody lost money somewhere — but it was a colossal operation: it was extraordinarily expensive to run. Bills were huge. So financially it failed. It didn't ultimately make a profit. But it proved something to me that I'd always believed which is that the problem with really creative music is that it must be attainable on more than one level.

For almost a year after Colosseum disbanded Hiseman was once more at the crossroads. During this period he worked with a few jazz groups and produced a few albums for other people. But most of the time seems to have been spent in intense self-examination. Although he has the reputation, among some musicians, of being pushy and arrogant, he is his own sternest critic, and is also quick to

recognise quality in other musicians — particularly drummers. Also during this period he allied himself with the
Musicians' Action Group, bringing a quick, incisive mind
and a wealth of practical experience to the various meet-
ings. His analysis of the current plight of jazz in Britain is
full of tough common sense:

> I don't think music, if it's to survive, can be very narrow. We
> must have, in any growing musical body, several elements
> flourishing simultaneously, and some elements must pay for
> others. The Action Group is complaining that there's no
> outlet for jazz, and the most militant complainers are the
> people playing the most outrageously avant-garde music.
> You can listen to John Stevens, Tony Oxley, Howard Riley,
> Barry Guy, Derek Bailey and co., and you can like it or dis-
> like it according to your taste. That's not an issue. What is at
> issue is that that music should exist and that people should
> have freedom to do it, but they must be able to earn a living
> because this society runs on money. If we were in a situation
> where there were some very good middle-of-the-road jazz
> bands playing whatever is acceptable today — a style full of
> panache and showbiz if you like, but playing music as valid
> now as Coltrane's was ten years ago, and if the record com-
> panies could make a profit on two albums a year from, say,
> five British bands, they would be willing to subsidise the
> more extreme avant-garde. This kind of subsidy happens in
> all the other areas of music. They make so much money
> from Beethoven's *Fifth* that they can put out other classical
> records which will never make money in a million years.
> And a company like Warner Brothers will make so much
> money out of Three Dog Night, or Humble Pie, or Deep
> Purple, or the Faces, that they can afford to pay a band like
> Colosseum £12,000 more than the band earn and so sub-
> sidise it. . . and Colosseum was relatively successful com-
> pared with many bands that receive large advances on the
> speculation that they will make money . . . and nobody turns
> round and asks you to pay the money back. In other words,

for any kind of healthy artistic thing, like a gallery, for instance, which is selling paintings and making a healthy profit, it's essential that it also sells paintings which make very little, or no, profit and therefore subsidises young or lesser well-known artists. What we've got in jazz is a situation where the musicians who want to be avant-garde — way ahead of the public — are not subsidised simply because there is no centre core of successful middle-of-the-road jazz. If we had a whole healthy cross-section going on, then the more accessible forms of the music would subsidise the more way-out forms and a natural balance would be found between the two.

Optimism, vision, and direction returned to Jon Hiseman in 1972 and he formed a new band called Tempest — a name which, like Colosseum, conjures up a vision of huge, inhuman energy, and suggests that whenever the band plays the performance is a larger-than-life event. The sense of occasion is borne out in Hiseman's final words:

As soon as I started playing to universities with a thousand people in the hall, I got infected by the communication with the audience which I'd never realised existed before . . . To walk out on a stage in, say, Berlin with an audience of like seven thousand people — they've been waiting for you all night and it's electric, and you've got to go out there and give them what they've come to expect — it's a tremendous challenge which now I couldn't do without . . . But at the same time I've become very conscious that I'm preparing myself for something, that what I'm doing is not the be-all and end-all of what I can achieve, that it's only a road and I don't know where it's going to lead or what it will lead to. But what I'm doing now is not the ultimate thing that I hope to be capable of; it's only a very narrow part. But I've been doing it for five years and I'm not finished yet. When I'm finished with it, then I will finish it.

6

EVAN PARKER

Saxophonist Evan Parker is a totally uncompromising radical experimentalist. He is respected by musicians of all persuasions as a master saxophonist and a man who is possibly creating a new language — or, rather, a new dialect of the jazz language. Certainly, the music Evan Parker makes with such close associates as Derek Bailey or Paul Lytton seems to bear very little relationship to the jazz tradition. The regular pulse, harmonic progressions and melodies which identify, clothe, support and stimulate the improvisations of most jazz to date, have all been dispensed with. Like John Stevens and Trevor Watts, Parker has done a sort of cultural striptease over the years since the mid–1960s, shedding one convention after another. And also like John Stevens, Parker does not attempt to dissociate himself from jazz even though some of his associates prefer to think of themselves as belonging more to the European musical tradition. Evan Parker asserts: "I still use the word 'jazz'. For me I'm playing jazz." A listener whose musical experience is limited to the mainstream jazz traditions might find that statement incredible faced with the totally unfamiliar sounds of his music. Parker explores the technical resources of the tenor and soprano saxophones to their limits; he uses harmonics so high that they are on bat frequencies; he sustains tensions

Evan Parker
London,
January 1974
(photo © Jak
Kilby).

for long periods, and plays extremely unusual melodic
shapes; he also splits up notes into their component parts
— the harmonics which form one normal saxophone note.
The resultant effect is possibly something like (if it could
be done) putting one bar of music under a very powerful
microscope or stethoscope. What we see or experience is
still music, but we are aware of the fibres of it, the component parts, the usually concealed physics, in extreme close-
up. But the continuity with the jazz tradition is there — it is
in the energy and intensity both of the feelings and of the
way they are expressed.

    In other words, although Parker's musical language
may seem strange and forbidding, in fact it is shot through

with the emotional heat of the blues and gospels, and with all the improvising fervour of the central jazz tradition. And he says: "I don't think you need special knowledge to listen to what we do . . . it's just for everybody, you know . . . As long as people don't think that because they don't know the rules they don't know what it's all about . . . that tends to be the problem."

It tends to be more of a problem in Britain than elsewhere, and Evan Parker seems to earn most of his income by playing on the Continent — particularly in Germany, where he has a big reputation. It may be that his complex personality and the disconcerting nature of his music are exciting to Continental audiences who are used to the idea of change and development, whereas to the British mentality which craves for the security of familiar territory his conception is too disturbing to be easily acceptable.

He certainly seems to be a mass of paradoxes. His playing appears to be wild and abandoned, but it is, in fact, extremely disciplined and controlled. Although his musical approach seems to suggest intellectual emotional anarchy, Parker has thought everything out — his music, his life, his attitudes — very clearly, and can express his thoughts in lucid, effortlessly succinct prose. Although his music makes no concessions to the consumer society, Parker is still fully aware that to make any impact, to get his message over, he has to use some of the techniques of the very society he is resisting . . . the publicity and exposure made possible by the media. When he's reminded how highly other musicians speak of him and how much in the forefront of their minds he is, he says: "Well, Derek [Bailey] might accuse me of seeking that!" And, of course, he is much more of the world than his close associate the fastidious and ascetic Derek Bailey, whose own striptease involved not only discarding conventional harmony and rhythm but also abandoning the whole jazz tradition of collective, communal music-making.

Derek Bailey's own particular endgame has caused him to withdraw into himself, and concentrate on playing solo guitar. The process of withdrawal seems to have taken place over several years, and to be marked by quite clearly defined stages; the years of playing bread-and-butter music in every branch of the musical entertainment industry were followed by some years of playing radically experimental group music in London and on the Continent. Bailey worked so much abroad that he could have made his home in Germany, but he declined most of the work he was getting and continued to live in England. He was rapidly arriving at the stage where he saw the nearest parallels to his own role in those of a writer or painter . . . He sees a kind of musical approach in some of the writings of Samuel Beckett — the juxtaposition and repetition of words in a musical way. So, like writers and painters who work alone, Bailey stopped looking for a collective outlet. He is austere, uncompromising and formidably committed to exploring and expressing his own interior vision, and he emits a sort of feeling that this vision would be deformed or tarnished if it were made to fit in with the exterior landscape of group music . . . at least on a regular basis. He enjoys playing occasionally with other people with whom he feels a strong affinity, but such people are few and far between. With monastic vigilance he tries to avoid the habitual side of playing.

Compared with this religious sense of purity, this sense of keeping an untainted vision, Evan Parker's approach is secular, agnostic, robust. He is prepared to rub shoulders and get involved with all sorts and conditions of musicians, and seems able to do this without losing his essential identity. It is because he associates regularly with other

Derek Bailey, London, November 1970 (photo © Jak Kilby).

musicians and because he can relate to their musical language and make them feel the power of his own language that he makes such an impact on such a variety of them. So his group musical activity can range from, say, playing solo saxophone, to playing duets with drummer Paul Lytton, to playing with one of Kenny Wheeler's big or small groups, or playing with Chris McGregor's Brotherhood of Breath. Evan Parker gets around, puts himself about, wants to be noticed, is glad of publicity, and is always totally dedicated to his conception of saxophone playing — which is appallingly original. So how did his conception evolve, where does he get his all-embracing, non-exclusive view of music, and how can he identify with so many different jazz variants and still keep his identity intact?

His early influences were the same as those of anyone else who became aware of music during the fifties. Pop music and the singles market got to him first, and he was excited by singers like Guy Mitchell and Frankie Laine, by instrumental records like Humphrey Lyttelton's *Bad Penny Blues* (and how many people did that record turn on?), and by Lonnie Donegan and the whole skiffle thing:

> I was absolutely fanatical about Lonnie Donegan. I just had everything that he ever recorded. I knew all the words and was very interested in that kind of music. I'd read that he was influenced by Leadbelly so I went into that. At that time there were two ten-inch LPs on Melodisc of Leadbelly and I think I heard the difference. I think that in a way I preferred the Donegan versions though in another way I knew the others were more important. It was just a question of allowing myself to mature to the point where I would feel it as well as understand the importance of it. There was very little of that stuff around. You could get one or two things on Tempo. There was Sonny Terry, Brownie McGhee . . . Josh White. You had to take what you could get . . . It was all single records really. One record was enough to lead you into the next thing. One Lonnie Donegan record was enough to lead you to Leadbelly and that was enough to make me check out the whole of the blues that was available which was about seven or eight records.

His interest broadened rapidly from skiffle and the blues to traditional jazz — Chris Barber and Louis Armstrong (the same reverse process . . . first the disciple and then the prototype) — and then to Dave Brubeck, Paul Desmond, and ultimately (when he was fourteen) to John Coltrane. And almost from the start he began playing music:

Playing was just a natural extension of listening to records.
If you get to a certain degree of involvement in the music
you just want to do it yourself and you don't care how bad it
is . . . I first started playing guitar with some sort of skiffle
group, but I never knew what choruses were or chord
changes. I thought, for example, when I listened to Dave
Brubeck that — and this is a shocking admission to make —
that when the tune stopped they just played whatever was
in their heads. I knew that there was some connection with
the tune, but nobody had told me that there was a chord
progression and that it all took place in a certain number
of bars. I suppose I was naive in that respect. I never got
anywhere with music at school. I was always very dull at that.
At the school I went to you could either do music or science
and I did science . . . So I knew I wasn't making it with the
guitar because I didn't know what chords were. But I knew
what a melody line was and I could play that on saxophone.
I was left £100 by a relative that died. I didn't know whether
to buy a racing bike — Claude Butler frame and all kinds of
foreign gears, special wheels, brakes and so on . . . you had
to put the whole thing together yourself like a custom-built
racing bike. I went and looked in the window of the shop,
and something stopped me. I thought: "No, I must buy a
saxophone." So I did that and I think I was robbed. I went
to this shop and they deliberately sold me a very old, far too
expensive saxophone. Then I was recommended a teacher
and I started to get some idea of the way harmonic music
worked. I started on the saxophone basically because I was
obsessed with Paul Desmond.

Evan Parker was lucky with his saxophone teacher, a man
called Jimmy Knott. It would seem that he taught not only
an instrument, but also a life-style. Parker comments:

He played in a circus — Chessingtons — just a miniature circus band — alto sax, accordion and drums. He had a big
sound on alto and he helped me a fantastic amount. He

used to make saxophone transcriptions of popular classical things. I remember we did some Tchaikovsky things from *Swan Lake*, and part of the *Pathétique Symphony*, some Bach and Mozart and all kinds of things. He would write out whatever you wanted him to, so he spent a lot of time writing out Paul Desmond solos, and we'd play those. Towards the end of the time I studied with him I asked him to do some Coltrane solos, but he wouldn't do that. I think it was too much work. But he'd do Charlie Parker solos, and he'd done a Joe Harriott solo off an old record. He was a pretty enlightened teacher and I went to him until I went to university, which was about four years.

He studied botany for two years at Birmingham University, and then dropped out of the course because his interest in music caused him to neglect his academic studies. Within two weeks of arriving at the university he was playing with a group of good musicians — piano, bass and drums and Evan on tenor sax — and it was his first experience of playing in a band with a really good rhythm feel. The pianist was Hywel Thomas, and he and the bass player were very much at home with harmonic sequences. The repertoire of the band was mostly from the then current John Coltrane albums on the Impulse label, and they included such things as *Afro-Blue*, and *My Favourite Things*. That was the beginning of Trane's modal period, and Parker says:

> The roles of the piano player and the bass were reduced. Both Hywel Thomas and the bass player didn't want to play on pedal notes and scales all night. So we played a repertoire that used changes as well as modality.

Of course, to a musician accustomed only to vertical improvisation on changing chord patterns it would seem that modal playing (extracting different chords from the same scale or series of notes) would be more limiting. In fact, playing on a mode or on a pedal or root requires a different order of sophistication and skill. Harmony becomes decorative instead of functional, and the use of space becomes an even more crucial factor in the music. Also the various structures of an improvisation and even the differing bar lengths can be determined by the musicians on the spur of the moment. Obviously, to make real use of this degree of freedom, musicians need to have considerable sophistication and sensitivity. Just as Hywel Thomas was rooted in chord changes and uninterested at that time in the potential of modal or horizontal improvising, so Evan Parker was more or less ignorant of chordal playing and leaning towards horizontal freedom. He describes the situation:

> I got interested in playing more freely, and Hywel could see that it made sense but he just couldn't bring himself to do it . . . I never really covered that area — change-playing. Though I do understand more about chords now than when I was actually trying to play them. I haven't studied them intensively. It's just that I'm more familiar with the instrument and I know how the patterns fall.

Because his father worked for BOAC, Evan Parker was able to get free flights to New York in 1961 and 1962. which afforded him first-hand experience of the American scene when he perhaps was most susceptible to its influence. Without a doubt, the intensity and commitment of the Americans he saw made a lasting impression on him:

> I saw everything, you know. I met Cecil Taylor and had a long conversation with him and that was about two weeks before he went to Denmark to work at the Montmartre Club. And I also talked to Sonny Murray and Jimmy Lyons for about two hours . . . they were with Taylor . . .When I arrived at the club, it was such a strange little place that I couldn't believe that Cecil Taylor was actually going to

come out and play, and I wouldn't buy a drink. Something inside me said that this was some kind of hype — a New York sort of hype — and they've just put Cecil Taylor's name outside and they want to sell me a drink and Cecil Taylor's not going to come on. So I wouldn't buy a drink until Cecil Taylor actually appeared. And then he appeared. And I couldn't believe it. And the barman came over and said: "Will you buy a drink now then? There he is!" To the guy selling the drinks there was this bum Cecil Taylor. And he was thinking, "Why is this guy so worked up about Cecil Taylor?" So anyway, he sold me the drink, and they played a set for about an hour and a half . . . that was a fantastic experience . . . just to sit there and be washed over by this free improvisation for an hour and a half.

Everything he saw in New York left a very vivid impression. Coltrane was still his strongest influence, but he was becoming aware of all sorts of other people and other areas . . . Carla Bley's composing . . . Gary Peacock's bass playing . . . Steve Lacy and Roswell Rudd playing Thelonious Monk's tunes. But perhaps the next most powerful revelation after Coltrane was Eric Dolphy:

> . . . That aspect of Dolphy's thing — the large intervals, and the sense of phrase . . . that thing where you can't tell whether a phrase is going up or down because it's doing both things at once. That movement away from the feeling that this is an ascending phrase and that is a descending phrase. I got that from some of the things that Cecil Taylor and Eric Dolphy were doing.

Although he got thrown out of the university after a couple of years Evan Parker hung around the place making use of the facilities and playing with the quartet. He explains the significance of this development:

> I suppose I was one of the first of the drop-out thing. Not many people were doing it then. I was quite capable of doing

the course but I just didn't do any work. I'd done my A levels at Chiswick Polytechnic which was then a very liberal
place, and the guy who had taught me there was a real
teacher. When I got to university I found they were all dead
and only interested in their own research anyway. It was a
weakness on my part I think, looking back. I would quite
like to have finished. It was the first time I'd ever failed anything really, apart from the cycling proficiency test, and I
think it's still with me in a way — the sense that I failed even
if it wasn't on my terms . . . But talking to guys who have
degrees, they're not sure whether having it gives them problems in music — like Nick Evans, for example . . . Having
the degree there is a piece of economic security which
means that any time you want to you can teach somewhere,
fall out and just give it all up if it gets too much. Nick's scared
he won't be so committed because he'll know in the back of
his mind that he's got that to fall back on. I haven't got that.
Music is it. I'm really committed to that. In a way, I'm glad
that I don't have the degree.

For two years after dropping out of the university course,
Parker carried on living in Birmingham and playing with
the same quartet. He got married, and he and his wife rent-
ed a house. Parker had about three regular gigs a week,
and augmented his earnings by doing non-musical work at
times. Also, at this time, he began to do some work with
Howard Riley who was then studying music at Bangor
University, but his home was in Birmingham and he spent
the vacations there. Evan Parker comments on the quartet's development:

We were using that approach where it's not clear whether
you're playing changes or scales, like Coltrane does on the
other side of *My Favourite Things* where he plays
Summertime and *But Not For Me*. I played changes but in
a sort of oblique way. We altered the original sequences of
things, and we also played straight ahead modal stuff as well.

Everybody was clearly with their influences, like me trying to sound like Coltrane, the piano-player trying to sound like McCoy Tyner, the drummer trying to sound like Elvin Jones, and the bass player just playing pedals. Then the trio would play by itself and try to sound like the Bill Evans Trio. We had the right influences, perhaps, even before those influences got to be strong on the scene as a whole. It took a while for the piano players in town [London] to pick up on Bill Evans, whereas Hywel was already into that.

It became clear, however, that there was no future for a dedicated jazz musician in Birmingham — just as there is no future for any such musician in any British provincial town. To develop his conception it was essential for Parker to go and live in London, but to do this he and his wife needed money enough to see them through the whole process of moving, flat-hunting, and creating a new life-style. For the first and probably the last time in his life, Parker took an ordinary job and tasted the kind of existence that most of the population experience:

I did ten months working the night shift at Cadbury's, doing all kinds of things with chocolate like wrapping it, and all the fascinating things that a man can do in a chocolate factory, I did. Then one morning on the way home they found large quantities of their chocolate in the pockets of my coat, and, assuming that I'd stolen it, they gave me the sack. I think if they hadn't given me the sack, I might have ended up there for life. I couldn't get out of it. I was hypnotised by the whole thing — drugged by it. I think I was late clocking in more times than anybody had ever been in the history of the organisation. They've got very loyal employees there, guys that had worked there for thirty years. You can work there for twenty years and your name doesn't even get in the special book . . . twenty-five years and your name goes in the book . . . thirty years and you get some kind of gold watch or something. That's a real heavy set-up. It's called the

'Factory in the Garden'. I used to say that you could see the factory from the garden, but you can't see the garden from the factory. I didn't enjoy it at all, but it trapped me.

Evan Parker came to London in 1965 or '66, and made straight for the Little Theatre Club. It was the obvious centre for new faces, the place to go to find out what was happening and what was available. The Ronnie Scott Club used to provide a similar service for established musicians — a grapevine service, and an after-hours meeting place. At first, Parker went to the Theatre Club to listen to the SME which at that time comprised John Stevens, Trevor Watts, Paul Rutherford, and the bass player Bruce Cale. But he eventually made himself known and joined the group. Almost immediately he spent three months in Denmark with John Stevens and Trevor Watts, an experience which, coming straight after the Birmingham scene, enlarged his perspectives with a shock:

> My wife was pregnant with our first kid and so she didn't come with us . . . It was a real big move for us. There were people there who had a very different attitude. Albert Ayler had been in Denmark a lot, and John Tchicai was living there. They were pretty powerful influences. So the guys there were playing freer than we expected. We thought we'd be taking a new message there and turning everybody on to this. We thought we were playing free — but we found the people there were playing freer things.

But this marked the beginning of Parker's extremely fruitful association with John Stevens. It can be safely said that when Evan Parker joined the SME and John Stevens, he was a promising young musician, and when their paths diverged two years later, he had established a powerful identity and a mature conception. He is the first to admit his debt to John Stevens:

John is a very demanding guy to work for. Exactly what you're doing is not always made clear, but the discipline of that period I found fitted me very well for every situation since. John put me in situations that nobody's put me in since in a way — like playing louder than I could play and playing quieter than I could play, to name just two of the most obvious problems that he set me. And he just sets you problems until you find a solution. I must say, I learnt a lot from John. In a way, our musical directions have diverged-completely since then, but I'm very glad about the period that we spent together.

Back in England, Parker went through all the phases of the SME during the later sixties, which meant working with groups which included at various times Kenny Wheeler, Derek Bailey, Paul Rutherford, Trevor Watts, Barry Guy, Chris Cambridge and Jeff Clyne. He did his first radio broadcasts with the SME, and he also established close relationships with some of the other members of the group . . . relationships which were to prove as vital as his association with John Stevens:

> . . . [The SME] put me in touch with Derek Bailey, which is quite one of the most important things that has happened to me musically. Derek and I had a sort of rehearsal duo at the time when we were playing in John's band, and I think, in a way, we were already formulating a divergence from John's trend of thought in free music. Tony Oxley was always somewhere there on the periphery — working at Ronnie Scott's Club but with an ear to what was going on because of his long association with Derek Bailey in Sheffield. They'd had a trio there with Gavin Bryars on bass. He's just a composer now, but he was a very good bass player in his time. So Tony was there as a presence as well, and I had some very nice plays with Tony at the Theatre Club in that period when we were not sure whether we were playing time or not.

I remember that Tony was quite a proposition too, but at
that time we didn't get much chance to play together — he
just came and sat in a couple of times.

All kinds of innovations seemed to be happening during
the later sixties. The SME was reduced to a duo — Evan
Parker and John Stevens . . . saxophone and drums, which
was in itself remarkable, and another shock for the conser-
vative jazz world. Throughout the period when he was
duetting with John Stevens, Parker always kept in touch
with Derek Bailey. At that time Bailey was living in Putney,
and Parker used to go there regularly to rehearse with him.
And Bailey himself was beginning to shake up conventional attitudes. He gave a solo guitar recital with prepared
tapes at the Old Place, at a time when playing solo jazz guitar was outside the bounds of anybody's thinking, The use
of prepared tapes was another innovation so far as jazz was
concerned, though John Cage had been using such things
for several years. But in some respects, the jazz experiments were well ahead of similar developments in the
'straight' music world. Parker comments, not without
some bitterness:

> At least a year before Stockhausen wrote the so-called intu-
> itive pieces which are just instructions about emptying the
> mind and not making any sounds until you hear the sounds
> that should be made, all those activities were things that the
> Little Theatre Club group of musicians were already doing.
> But because the culture machine works for the composer
> and works for the academies of music, then this whole
> stream of ours lacks that kind of cultural acceptance.

The irony is that Parker and Bailey were well aware of
key developments on the straight scene and had enough
perspective to be able to relate their own work to that
scene. Parker explains:

The influence that straight music has had on me has been through certain works which have been germinal for me. And I've felt that if I've heard *that* work I don't need to hear all the works which are simply that same thing in another form. One of the first things was *Le Marteau Sans Maître,* the Boulez piece, which I heard on the radio. *Malone Dies* was just out in paperback. I sat there reading *Malone Dies* in the afternoon in my digs with my landlady bringing me cups of tea, and listening to *Le Marteau Sans Maître* on the radio. There was one version of it you could buy on record, that was the Robert Craft one in the Philips series, and I went out and ordered it from the record shop immediately. That influenced me for a whole period after that. The musical ideas I took from that would have been expressed in the period of the duo with John Stevens, and where we made the *Karyobin* album with Kenny Wheeler, Dave Holland, Derek, John and myself. It's filtered through that jazz consciousness or whatever you like to call it, but it's that kind of approach — interrelated lines, interlocked structures. Of course, in Boulez it's derived from incredibly complex mathematical procedures. The sleeve note mentioned the magazine *Die Reihe*, the Stockhausen-edited thing, and I followed that through. That was an incredibly biassed pro-serial magazine . . . it was the whole post-Webernian school where they thought they detected in Webern, elements of serialisation of other parameters than pitch, so they thought that that was the next phase of the music — to serialise the other parameters formally. If you see the early lines of Webern it's not quite serialised. You'll have a melody line that's eleven notes without anything repeated, but not the series, then there'll be a repetition before he completes the series . . . when serialist theory evolved everything tightened up. There could be wrong notes: "Ah, is this a serialist piece? Because if it is, then this is a wrong note, because that's presumably the so-and-so inversion and if that's the case, this should be a D sharp!" So there was a whole new

way of saying: "Ha! Ha! You're wrong!" But I didn't tumble
to that for a while, so I believed everything in *Die Reihe*. So
Le Marteau was an important piece for me. Then later on, I
heard *Transition 2* by Mauricio Kagel which I found very
interesting . . . and also the *Sonatas* and *Interludes for
Prepared Piano* by John Cage . . . I don't listen to these
things for their realisation of formal concepts but only to
the way they work as sounds, because I don't have that
academic training. I've pieced a vocabulary together so that
I can talk to people that do have that training, but it's not a
natural thing for me to do.

Because of their growing interest in contemporary
straight music, Evan Parker and Derek Bailey began to col-
laborate with some of the musicians from that scene. At
first, they formed a group with Gavin Bryars who spe-
cialised in amplification and the use of electronics. He was
also a very useful source of information about contemporary developments because he'd spent all his university
grants on contemporary scores, and had amassed a fairly
comprehensive collection. Eventually, John Tilbury the
pianist and drummer Jamie Muir were added to the group
which was intended to play contemporary works that the
members liked and to improvise as well. Evan Parker
describes some of the problems:

> Gavin was beginning to develop an ideological objection to
> improvisation. He would make the programmes over-run
> so that the improvisation, which had been scheduled as
> the last set, would never get played. We'd be playing those
> indeterminate pieces like a Cage piece or a George Brecht
> piece with radios, whatever Gavin felt like . . . they'd come
> up with the recommendation for pieces. We did some
> Cornelius Cardew things and any score that they recom-
> mended because of . . . their better background, really . . .
> I mean Tilbury's the father of that sort of thing in England
> in terms of performance. I think Derek and I were learning

all the time in that situation, but also, we were not being allowed to improvise. We had to stop that. Then after that, we played as a trio — Jamie, me and Derek, and I was working with a contact mike on the saxophone at that time. Jamie was working with some form of amplification on parts of his kit, and Derek was exploring the possibilities of his instrument as they say. That was a nice trio. We added Hugh Davies later, which seemed a natural thing to do. Hugh's an ex-assistant of Stockhausen . . . not from the jazz scene at all. He really doesn't know much about it, but we found that an advantage . . . like Cecil Taylor said about bass players, that he'd much prefer to play with those that think they can't play. That was what was most useful to him at that early stage . . . Hugh is on the Music Improvisation Company record, and that developed pretty well, I think . . . By this time we'd developed an ideological bias against composition almost in any form . . . I don't know if the Music Improvisation Company exists at all now, but it's nobody's first impulse . . . Victor Schonfield still believes in it and occasionally finds attractive jobs for it and we do them. It happens about twice a year. Finally we added a voice — a girl called Christine Jeffrey . . . she's a painter, sculptor, and I think the voice for her is a natural extension of those kinds of activity, so she has no musical preconceptions at all. We had the trio there, and then we added Hugh who wasn't sure whether he was a technician or a musician (I think he'd probably resent that), but he certainly wasn't from the jazz tradition anyway . . . then the culmination of that line of thought was. . . Derek and I were in a pub one night. Peter Kowald had come over from Germany, and there was this amazing old homosexual in the bar there . . . very old . . . completely past it, but he knew he was past it . . . Kept making these advances to Kowald, this great muscular, heavy German. We thought he did it so well. He put these routines and patter in between these advances, and kept muttering about: "If we'd been in the Navy together!"

all this sort of stuff, and: "Oh, let me feel your arm again."
We were falling about, and we thought, "This guy's got to
come on the next gig with us" . . . We offered him the gig
but he said: "No! Certainly not! I'm not going to do that!"
He said: "You can come to my room sometime and hear me
sing. I do light opera. Come to my room in the afternoon.
But I'm not coming with you. Falmouth? Don't be ridicu-
lous!" That was where the gig was. That was, for me, the end
of the dynamic of the Music Improvisation Company
although we've done two gigs since then in a period of about
eighteen months, and they've both been fantastic gigs. But
the strain . . . they take everything from you, from the body,
from the mind, everything, and it drained you completely.
There's total demand from everyone. And my feeling is that
the band can't work more than twice a year anyway because
of its peculiar alchemy. Five is already quite a lot of people
to be playing absolutely free together, and when it's those
five it really stretches in every direction and it's very tense.
But at the same time it's very creative, it seems to me.

When the Old Place was finally closed, there was once
more no real playing outlet for young British
musicians. During its eighteen months of life, the Old
Place had spawned a very lusty crop of musicians who had
developed a kind of self-respect that was new to the British
scene. They knew they were good, and, not just one or two
leading lights, but everybody had increased expectancies
about the amount of work they should have. The Jazz
Centre Society was set up to deal with this situation . . . to
find places for regular weekly sessions, and to receive
financial aid from the Arts Council. A group of musicians
involved in the more extreme forms of radical experimen-
tation believing that the Jazz Centre Society was discrimi-
nating against them and their music, broke away and
formed the Musicians' Co-operative. At first the membership included John Stevens and Trevor Watts, but they

eventually found the Co-op too isolationist and they refused to sever their ties with the Jazz Centre Society. So the basic membership of the Co-op was, in effect, the Little Theatre group of musicians without Stevens and Watts. In other words, the Musicians' Co-op was mostly comprised of people who had developed out of the SME: Evan Parker, Derek Bailey, Barry Guy, Howard Riley, Tony Oxley, Paul Rutherford and Paul Lytton. Parker describes some of its functions:

> When we started the Co-op, it was much more of a socio-political expression than a musical one. There was no musical coherence within the Co-op. There wasn't an aesthetic grouping as such, except that we all tended to be from the freer end of the spectrum. But amongst ourselves we have violent disagreements about music. It's very hard for Tony Oxley to convince me that his compositions are necessary,

Barry Guy
(photo
Contemporary
Music
Network /
Arts Council).

and even harder for him to convince Derek. And Derek plays solo now . . . that's an expression of something. And Barry Guy has a big band which he writes for and he gets almost ridiculed for that by other members of the Co-op. Well, he's subjected to heavy humour for the mere act of making an arrangement, for imposing those parts on other people. Yet, when you have a guy like Paul Lytton in a meeting . . . whatever anybody says, there's always a point that's completely different and Paul usually finds that. So there's no coherence; it's just that we are learning to understand one another. It's as much a psycho-therapeutic exercise for us as it is a practical way of handling our social problems as musicians.

Whatever the rights and wrongs of the situation, the Co-op has made certain very valid contributions to the scene in general. It has put on regular concerts at the Cockpit Theatre, the Ronnie Scott Club (on Sunday nights), and occasional concerts at other places. It has also given regular jolts to the complacency of other musicians and other organisers. By persistently setting up ideal hypotheses it has offered a steadily continuous criticism of the real conditions and attitudes of the scene. Its danger, and perhaps its main weakness, is that because it is always setting itself up as the conscience of the jazz scene in general, it tends towards self-righteousness . . . which means, of course, that it tends to be guilty of the very failing it is fighting against — a lack of self-criticism. It may be that the formation of the Musicians' Action Group has made the wider significance of the Co-op redundant. This is because the Action Group cuts across existing divisions and represents such a broad section of musicians that the self-criticism comes from within, not from outside. This makes the dangers of self-indulgence and self-righteousness much less likely to occur. But for its members, the Co-op seems to continue to offer a fairly comprehensive way of getting to grips with their situation and problems. Evan Parker points out that one of his main concerns is that he doesn't want anything to interpose itself between him and his audience. The audience is very important to him; he doesn't want it to be increased and built up by the kind of image projection which the hype-merchants of rock music go in for; in other words, he doesn't want his music to be sold as anything other than a sound. The irony is that music can never be only a sound if it is made by and heard by humans. Also, not to want an image is in itself an image. In fact, Evan Parker does very well in projecting his image which is that of a left-wing purist rebelling against the cheap and squalid commercialism of the consumer society. More and more, through the developments of the rock scene, this kind of image is becoming popularly accepted and . . . irony of ironies . . . a highly economic proposition.

The Co-op is, in fact, a way of taking care of business until a suitable middleman or agent can be found. To this end, they have already formed their own record label (Incus) and publishing company. Parker explains:

> They don't exactly belong to the Co-op, but it looks like they're going to be used by most of the guys . . . Technically, the company belongs to Tony, Derek and myself, and not to the other members of the Co-op. We have a kind of financial adviser and backer, but he's not involved in the musical policy at all. He just helps us with the accounts and that kind of thing . . . his name is Michael Walters. I don't see the point in making a record for an organisation like CBS or RCA because when music like ours gets recorded, only a minority audience is ready for it when it first comes out. But maybe when it's been around for a year, a few more people are ready for it . . . but by that time a big company would have deleted it because the accounting department would have laid down rules about minimum sales required for an album to stay in the catalogue . . . our own records aren't

treated like that. We'll always keep a small number available in the stocks, like Blue Note records did. In practice, we sell to anybody who wants to buy . . . by post . . . we export records directly ourselves. The Jazz Composers' Association works for us in the US and Canada. The Instant Composers' Pool works for us in Holland. The Free Music Production and ECM work for us in Germany. Most of these links are mutual . . . we work for them here . . . We haven't tied up the idea of mutual publishing yet. It takes a long time for things to come through from foreign rights . . . maybe three years, whereas if you have a mutual arrangement with a publishing company they come through in the same year — almost the same as royalties in this country. It's all a question of finding ways not to have this money out there in credit because credit's no use to us. It's happening slowly. I think this relates to a change in consciousness which is worldwide — or at least in areas where jazz is involved. There is a move towards decentralisation, based, I think on a loss of faith in the international companies. It's an expression of basic socialist attitudes like workers control, and also a rejection of the depersonalised, anti-human relationships that global companies tend to generate.

To put Evan Parker's situation in clear perspective is not a simple matter. He is first and foremost a virtuoso saxophonist and a radical experimentalist. But at the same time he seems rooted in the emotional core of jazz, and he is also happy to play in some of the groups (e.g. the Brotherhood of Breath) which base their music on the broad musical spectrum of the whole jazz tradition — which, in other words, use harmonies, regular rhythmic pulses and patterns, and diatonic melodies, as well as free improvisation, and irregular or non-existent pulses. Although Parker is in opposition to the stereotype world of the consumer society, he is prepared to use some of the techniques of that society to project his image and his music. Although he is deeply suspicious of business and businessmen, he is part of the Co-op which is an attempt to organise the affairs of its seven members in a practical and businesslike kind of way. In short, Parker's music is difficult, but he is at pains to make people aware of it — to give them the opportunity of getting used to it. So how does he make out financially? Evan Parker explains:

> My wife has always been my sponsor. She works, so when I'm not earning anything she carries us through . . . she's a teacher. But it's not a drag for her to do it. She likes it very much. I don't know whether I should feel: "Now's the time for me to be a man and support my wife and children," but I don't feel like that . . . I really feel that what I'm doing is important enough for me not to behave like a 'man' in that sense of the word. She certainly goes along with that. She doesn't feel that I'm copping out from my responsibilities. She knows that I actually work very hard . . . a lot harder than if I just took a job in an office and just went in there and drowsed and looked at my watch and made a few notes on a piece of paper . . . the civil service type of job . . . I work much harder than that. I don't stop . . . you know, the hours aren't nine till five . . . it's work the whole time, but then it's also leisure the whole time. It's a different lifestyle . . . you can't divorce work from play. I think that's the useful thing. I think that the family benefits from one of the people being in that type of situation. In fact, I've always earned something . . . Actually, when I left Birmingham I was doing quite well up there because I had three regular gigs a week, and when I came to London, my earnings dropped a bit. They've picked up in a straggly sort of way since then and, well, they're above the Birmingham level now . . . they're a bit less than a docker's or a bank clerk's, but we get by.

7

CHRIS McGREGOR

The Brotherhood of Breath

Chris McGregor is a big man with a smile like a satyr and an affable disposition — a kind of easy-going warmth that comes from sticking close to mother nature, and having a clear idea of man's place in the natural order of things. In fact, he lives with his family in a house deep in the Sussex countryside — not too far away from John Surman — and commutes from there to gigs elsewhere in Britain and abroad. Puffing his pipe, wearing a tattered straw hat, with his humorous blue eyes and a solid belly-laugh, he seems more like a jolly farmer than a virtuoso jazz pianist and the leader of one of the most volatile big bands in the business . . . the Brotherhood of Breath.

If one of the most important cultural aspects of jazz is the way it fuses Western and non-Western cultural elements,* then McGregor and the Brotherhood are uniquely placed to realise this fusion. How far they have really succeeded in doing so, of course, will have to be decided by musicologists and historians at a later date. The Brotherhood includes three outstanding African musicians — Dudu Pukwana the alto saxophonist, Mongezi Feza the

---

*Vide *Pop Music and the Blues* by Richard Middleton, Chapter 2 'Some Aspects of the Blues' for a detailed analysis of the relationship of the two cultures.

Chris McGregor (photo Jazz Centre Society).

trumpeter, and Louis Moholo the drummer. McGregor himself was born and brought up in South Africa, where his father taught in a Church of Scotland mission school. They lived in the Transkei province and were one of the only two white families in an area of ten square miles. This meant that McGregor's earliest musical experiences were of the music of the Xhosa tribespeople and the hymns sung in the mission church, many of which were composed by Christianised tribespeople, as well as the *Hymns Ancient and Modern* of standard Scottish Calvinism. From the very first, in other words, Chris McGregor was subjected to the influence of both cultures — the literate, verbal, intellectual and puritanical culture of the West, and the physical, instinctual, oral, more directly sensuous culture of the non-West (in this case, Africa).

In a sense, Chris McGregor was subjected to undiluted doses of both cultures in a quite remarkable way. The mission school represented Western culture in its most concentrated and vigorous form, and the picture was filled out considerably when McGregor went to the Cape Town College of Music and spent four years studying there. And his daily studies of the Western European musical tradition were augmented virtually every evening when he would be playing jam sessions in local jazz clubs with white and African musicians. McGregor gives some impression of the hectic activity of that period:

> Improvisation was natural to me, whereas those around me (at college), who were better trained really, were stumbling. I could improvise solutions to problems in the harmony class or the composition class, that the others had to slave over for two hours of homework. And then I'd be impatient. I'd improvise my solutions and then rush off to one of the clubs where things were happening and jam all night, get to the class in the morning, play my solution, and lose interest in the rest of the lesson! . . . Dollar Brand was running Sunday night sessions at a dancing school and I was playing there. Capetown was the Mecca of African jazz in 1957. The whole weekend was spent in the place rehearsing . . . there'd be dancers in one corner, weight-lifters and boxers in another corner, and then groups of people sitting around and drinking and chatting. This dancing school was in the part of Capetown that wasn't racially classified — so coloured and white could mix freely . . . At college I was respected by the teachers because I could do everything that was required of me. I was so used to depending on my ear that I didn't have many technical or theoretical hang-ups. I had a Debussy phase and a Bartók phase . . . got very deeply into Bartók and played the *Mikrokosmos* pieces and studied the concerto for two pianos and percussion. I was knocked out by him, and still am. Schoenberg — I did the first South African performance of his little suite for piano, *Opus 33A*. I was playing some Webern too — the variations.

This was pluralism with a vengeance. But McGregor was in no doubt as to where his real musical direction and

interest lay. When he left college he began playing with a
trio at a restaurant. It was a place for whites, but he could
use coloured musicians. He also played at a coffee
bar, and occasionally augmented the trio with horns . . .
played either by friends from the dance school sessions
or students from the college. But the scope of McGregor's
musical activity began to expand rapidly. There was actually a social need for the music . . . he explains what was
happening:

> People were trying a lot of different ways of promoting things
> . . . There was a new fire in the land . . . it was reaching out
> in all kinds of directions. We'd find ourselves going to play
> concerts in one of the further-out suburbs, you know,
> Newlands or somewhere, and coming back to the coffee bar
> (it was called the Vortex) and doing a set there . . . there was
> a growing audience for the music . . . there wasn't really
> much else on the go . . . it wasn't until the advent of the
> guitar groups that there was anything much else alive going
> on . . . and also it had nice cultural links with all kinds of
> other things . . . you never had to struggle to find a singer,
> you know.

At that time there was no real purist distinction between
kinds of music, and a jazz group could appear on the same
concert as, say, a vocal group doing barbershop harmony.
In fact, it was under exactly these circumstances that
McGregor first met Dudu Pukwana. The McGregor band
was asked to play at the opening of a youth cultural centre
in the African township of Capetown, and one of the other
acts was a vocal group called the Four Yanks which had
just blown in from Port Elizabeth. McGregor takes up the
story:

> The pianist playing with them struck me immediately, so I
> collared him afterwards: "Hallo, where do you come from?
> What's happening? How did you get to play like that? . . .

WOW! . . . It's nice! . . . Have a drink!" and that was Dudu! The first thing he said was: "I just wanted to come to Capetown, you know, and these guys were coming . . . but I like playing alto . . ." We found out we'd been listening to a lot of the same things . . . so he came and stayed with us and we started working as a quartet.

By 1963 Louis Moholo had joined the band on drums and Mongezi Feza had come in on trumpet, and the group was beginning to get fairly well known. But notoriety was a double-edged weapon in South Africa. Things were beginning to tighten up and for a mixed band like the McGregor outfit, there began to be a correlation between the amount of fame they had and the amount of pressure they could expect from the authorities. The thing was not to stand still — that just invited attention:

> We really hit the road with a vengeance. For about a year and a half we were constantly on the move — never staying in any place anywhere for more than about two weeks . . . and even that short stay would be a luxury . . . All the logistics had to be taken care of by my wife and me, and that was causing me a lot of dissatisfaction . . . You don't only have to cope with the normal touring hang-ups, you have to cope with the complete apartheid structure which means that you land in a place and find either that you're all sleeping in one place and putting someone at risk, or else you're staying ten miles apart and losing contact to that extent.

A way out came when Jacques Souplet, the man who runs the Antibes Jazz Festival, heard a tape of the McGregor band and asked them to appear at the festival. They played the festival and then knocked around on the Côte d'Azur until their money ran out:

> Then we made the best street band you've ever heard! We absolutely blasted the competition off the streets of Nice! The guys playing *When the Saints Go Marching In* with a

clarinet and a guitar, you know, they had no chance against us! We had nice three-horn arrangements of *Stomping at the Savoy, In the Mood* . . . I spent my last thirty francs on a guitar, then we went out collecting! And we made bread that way that I've only recently started to equal!

But that kind of easy money was bound to end with the summer. It's not just that the Côte d'Azur loses its tourists in the winter, but the local population all catch colds and influenza and these afflictions banish that openhearted gaiety which characterises the mad summer months. The Côte d'Azur is a quiet, thoughtful and rather mournful place out of season. These sort of facts began to make an impact on Chris McGregor and his band, but as usual, just when the good times seemed to be ending, when they seemed to be running out of luck, and were beginning to wonder if they would have to return to Africa, a call came from their old friend and mentor, the pianist Dollar Brand. He had preceded them to Europe and had already played some part in getting them to the Antibes Festival in the first place. Dollar Brand was at that time sharing with the blues singer Champion Jack Dupree the top spot at the Afrikaaner Cafe in Zürich. McGregor describes the kind of jazz scene going on at this cafe:

It would start at noon and go on till midnight or later, and involve about five different bands! . . . Champion Jack and Dollar wanted to do some travelling, so they reckoned it would be a good change of programme if there was a six-piece band for one part of the daily session anyway . . . Well . . . God Bless Dollar! . . . For four months we just went back and forth between the Afrikaaner Cafe in Zürich and the Blue Note in Geneva . . . doing a month in each place alternately . . . Then we were stuck in Zürich for nearly a year playing in that cafe for only nominal wages, and it was very hard work. We did two sessions a day there — 5 p.m. to 7 p.m., and then 9 p.m. to midnight . . . Heavy going if you want to do the occasional rehearsal! Also we began to get tired of living in German-speaking Zürich, and we wanted to speak to people in English for a change . . . So when we got invited to do two weeks at Ronnie Scott's Club, we jumped at the chance!

So in 1965 Chris McGregor's Blue Notes burst on the London scene. The news that some new musicians were in town buzzed around on the bush telegraph and most musicians got down to Scott's old club in Gerrard Street to have a listen . . . and a look. It was a band of powerful personalities ranging from the diminutive and quicksilver Mongezi on trumpet to the massively passionate Dudu Pukwana on alto sax. Johnny Dyani was on bass, and the rest of the rhythm section was, of course, Louis Moholo on drums, and Chris McGregor himself on piano. Their music had its own strongly individual flavour even then, but it seemed to come out of the Horace Silver/Art Blakey sort of school, though the McGregor band gave the impression of being much wilder and more abandoned than the Jazz Messengers.

Two or three years previously, before he'd left South Africa, McGregor had been laid up for almost a year after suffering from jaundice, and during his long period of recuperation he'd studied Ornette Coleman's records, which had just started to arrive in Africa. So, although, or perhaps even because, he was fully acquainted with the whole jazz tradition, he began to look for new musical directions. There was, in 1965, still no really established British scene, but the embryo was there. McGregor soon became friendly with John Stevens who was already deeply involved in his own quest for areas of new development. Naturally, when Stevens started the Little Theatre Club, the McGregor band played there.

The Blue Notes making their London debut at the ICA, London, 1965.
Left to right: Louis Moholo (drums), Johnny Dyani (bass), Chris
McGregor (piano), Dudu Pukwana (alto), Mongezi Feza (trumpet). Photo
© Val Wilmer.

Like Mike Gibbs, Chris McGregor came to England
with the beginnings of an international reputation. He had
already made some impact in Europe, and so it was not
surprising that his European connections continued, albeit
spasmodically, to flourish. In 1966 he and the band were
invited to play for four weeks at the Montmartre Club
in Copenhagen where John Stevens, Trevor Watts and
Evan Parker followed on after him. And it must be
remembered that Stevens and Watts also had the beginnings of a European reputation when they came to live in
London in the early '60s, after their stint with the RAF in
Germany. For McGregor as well as for Stevens, Watts and
Parker, the Copenhagen experience left a deep and lasting
impression. At that point, the McGregor band was ready

for change. Up to then, McGregor had spent most of his energies in organising the logistics of the band, and the composing had been done mainly by Dudu Pukwana. With a month's residency, McGregor was freed from organisational tyranny, and could devote his mind entirely to the music. He takes up the story:

> We'd been playing Dudu's repertoire, his tunes, for three years, and at Copenhagen we were at the Montmartre for a month and it was something of a breakthrough . . . in all kinds of directions. Albert Ayler and Archie Shepp had just been at the club, and Don Cherry and J. C. Moses, and Cecil Taylor was there for a month or two. That music was very much in the air. I was becoming conscious of a lot of things in myself . . . my own piano-playing was taking directions that weren't going to suit that old repertoire. Physically and technically I was reaching in all kinds of directions . . . especially Albert Ayler and his approach to tenor-playing opened up that whole thing to me. The muscular relationships would obviously appeal to somebody orientated to African music which is so much a dance . . . a body with muscles and sinews. It is so much a music of reaction and rhythm — the response of the body to rhythm. I saw how much Albert's music was very much *that* in this setting of Western civilisation . . . a way of keeping that flame alive . . .

It seems that following in the wake of such people as Albert Ayler and Cecil Taylor made McGregor profoundly aware — or confirmed him in his awareness — that the non-Western elements in jazz are supremely important. It is the fact of that fusion I described earlier which is the key to the music's identity. Suddenly Chris McGregor wanted to establish this close physical relationship with his instrument, to absorb it so much that it became as much a part of him as his voice . . . as much a part of his self-expression as language or gesture:

> I began doing an awful lot of practising on my own. I really wanted to establish my own physical relationship with my own instrument to a much deeper extent than before . . . It wasn't a sudden change . . . it was a deepening of an existing relationship. That was my particular obsession at that time . . . finding out what exactly I could do . . . me and this piano . . . Every instrumentalist at some stage in his career has to find out what his limits are really. The interesting thing is that as soon as you start doing that you increase your scope. You find out that your limits are really nowhere! . . . I always have to explore musical concepts physically and aurally.

Back in England, McGregor functioned with either a quintet or a sextet (adding Ronnie Beer on tenor sax) and concentrated on uncompromising experiment in the Ayler/Shepp vein. The tremendous energy was there and also the essence of that musical school . . . the 'funk seen through a glass darkly'. It was also during this period that the various apocryphal stories began to circulate — the legends of the McGregor band. Whether they are true or false is unimportant. Their significance lies in the fact that the people who recited them wanted to believe them . . . because the stories emphasise the uncontrollable, unpredictable, non-Western aspects of the band. There's the Bangor University story. The band arrived two hours late and without apology or explanation. went on stage and played flat-out for ten minutes of violent cacophony, and then went back to the dressing room. The distraught student organiser rushed to the dressing room and asked why they'd played so little and whether they could go back on immediately, only to be brushed aside by the McGregor statement: "Man, there's a lifetime's music in that ten minutes."

Again, a McGregor big band, so the story goes, turned
up late for a concert in Newcastle-on-Tyne, but once on
stage wouldn't stop playing and continued to roar out their
music as the audience slowly dwindled — trickling out to
catch the last bus home. But despite a growing reputation
and one or two good press notices, McGregor was still not
able to record regularly. It was not until he started leading
a bigger band, which eventually became called the
Brotherhood of Breath, that his development began to be
documented regularly on record. And he was ready by this
time to make his first really personal statements. He had
absorbed the various influences, he'd got to new grips with
the piano, and the big band needed a totally fresh and different repertoire . . . just at the moment when he was ready
to write new things. He explains how and why he started
the band:

> I've always been interested in bigger bands. I kind of enjoy
> the art of the energy-flow of a big band. I like the diversity
> of directions . . . a lot of different natural rhythms have to
> jell. I like the kind of energy you can generate that way . . .
> All jazz musicians have been exploring the relationship of
> superimposed rhythms and a steady pulse, and I feel that the
> relationship can go a lot further than most people think it
> can . . . and that's the general direction of my musical think-
> ing right now. The thing about a steady pulse is that it can be
> stated in so many different ways . . . and the art lies in keep-
> ing the pulse as interesting as you can, and with a drummer
> like Louis [Moholo] that's the easiest thing in the world
> because he's so incredibly inventive that he can keep it all
> alive . . . and that's what interests me . . . And another thing
> about the Brotherhood of Breath is that it's a way of getting
> the business together . . . I'm the kind of guy who likes to
> try and find a good sound economic basis for all cultural
> manifestations . . . and I find with the new music that I'm

more likely to have the seriousness of my bona fides accepted if I'm making myself responsible for thirteen people than
if I was making myself responsible for only four or five . . .
accepted by people who would be interested in promoting
us . . . It doesn't mean I'm selling out or anything like
that — I have the feeling that the only jazz musician who's
ever really had a consistent artistic and commercial thing
going at the same time is Duke Ellington. That aspect of his
life and career is a shining example. It's something to aim
at . . . Some musicians can thrive on flitting about from
group to group, and they can drop a beautiful gem here and
another one there, but I find that I'm not that kind. I thrive
on really steady relationships, and that applies right through
the band to the audiences and the people that I'm dealing
with, I tend to like relationships that stand for a kind of lifetime project . . . the ease of pace of steady relationships and
the kind of strength that they breed . . . I'm a Capricorn
native you know . . . you like to have your general relationships and your business relationships as clear as possible so
that you can give your mind to other things — and do all the
practising and composing that you want to do.

Chris McGregor was the first big band leader of the new
generation who is as powerful a soloist as any of his sidemen. By the end of the '60s he had developed a formidable piano technique, and seemed to have an inexhaustible
supply of ideas and rhythmic devices. Whatever else the
piano might be, with McGregor it was certainly a percussive instrument with enormous resources. The
Brotherhood had to be a 'blowing' band — a band which
did not rely heavily on written arrangements but which
gained its identity and strength from the improvising power
of its members. But there still had to be some kind of delicate balance between what was written or predetermined
and what was improvised. McGregor explains some of the
points and problems:

. . . The musicians in the Brotherhood have a very great deal of freedom. I'm against a doctrinaire division between writing and playing. Some things get written down after they are played — a great deal do — that effort of writing it down helps you to remember it . . . But writing music has a lot of validity because it's an easy way for certain basics to be transmitted — to be agreed on . . . especially for someone like Dudu with an African tradition of music behind him, it provides a good way of bridging the gap between himself and people with a European background. I find it works the same way for me and can be a means of quick communication . . . but that's not to forget that 'writing' music can simply take the form of suggesting a structure on which to improvise . . . and the structure can often be communicated verbally — in other words, it doesn't even have to be written down . . . and people compose while they're playing, of course . . . We don't any more play variations on versions of a song by, say, Irving Berlin. We play our own songs and there are places where it is impossible to say that that's precomposed or that's improvised . . . Musical structure is going to work itself out with whatever means are expedient to help it. . . Of course, a music that is totally improvised could conceivably be better structured than a piece written out note by note from beginning to end . . . I think it's a definite responsibility in the newer music that you have to be aware all the time that what you are improvising is the structure.

To a man of Chris McGregor's wide range of experience, there are no artificial barriers to music, and musical purism has no meaning. Whatever works is good. Whatever has quality, regardless of genre, is to be cherished. It is a long trip from the tribal music of Africa, the hymns of the mission school, the music of the romantics and classics, to the jazz influences of Parker and the other moderns. Also, when you have been reasonably well-off in South Africa, destitute in the South of France, over-worked in Switzerland, exposed in Copenhagen, and subjected to the testing dereliction of the philistine British, you tend to have a fairly balanced view of what is meaningful and desirable for you. And McGregor had one final yardstick by which to judge all experience. He has been at the mercy of the South African state . . . an individual feeling the weight of society's disapproval. And he has also experienced the hospitality for one whole week of a millionaire in the Bahamas who wanted to make a blues album, and hired McGregor and Alexis Korner to help him. In other words, McGregor has already felt the weight of intense collective and individual power. After these kinds of experiences, it's not surprising that despite the legends about the unpredictability and the crazy behaviour of the McGregor band, in fact one of Chris McGregor's main characteristics is a massive common sense. He puts the musical genres in perspective:

> In my own background I have classical music and still enjoy playing a lot of it, but I'm perfectly well aware that if I play a piece by Chopin it's a piece he went travelling around with in his own repertoire . . . and that it's *him* really, whereas what I'm building is *mine*. I haven't bothered with much rock music since Jimi Hendrix actually . . . Rock is just music — it's either good or bad . . . I think Jimi Hendrix's music is wonderful! . . . I can still listen to the Stones and get a kick out of that . . . The kind of fight that I have for respect, acceptance, economic stability and all the rest of it is quite solidly based on the assumption that if your economic stability is a matter of the number of people who'll listen to your music and the amount of money they'll spend, well, that's it! I'm in that marketplace too! And if it's a pop group we're playing opposite, they'd better do it! We've had some pretty revealing experiences, like playing an Implosion concert at the Roundhouse after three rather slow, boring, repetitive pop groups and really just waking that place up!

Like . . . we got the audience on their feet! Now for someone who's thinking in clichés of what pop music's about and
what avant-garde jazz is about and has got everything neatly
pigeonholed, that's a complete turnaround! . . . Which it
isn't for me . . . we went there to get them jumping and we
did! It's as simple as that! . . . Our economic struggle is a
matter of getting that through to people who do think in such
clichés. You find a thing like that isn't followed up, whereas
if our faces fitted or we played guitars or something I imagine that would have been good for one hell of a recording
contract and probably about three years of solid touring . . .
after just that one thing! . . . which then means that it's a
business conspiracy that you're fighting. And that's where
the categories are actually dangerous I think . . . the pigeonholing of music. Because then, of course, having engen-
dered that kind of energy and not having a follow-up, you've
got to do it all over again! . . . That's where the business
conspiracy and the pigeonholing are definitely an anti-life
thing, anti-culture, anti-everything! . . . It's an essential part
of the health of a music to have people who want to pay to
hear it — in the circumstances of Western civilisation anyway, because that's how the culture works . . . of course it
would be marvellous if we could be travelling around just
being taken care of by people who regarded the kind of
thing that we manifest as being of prime importance to their
cultural life! . . . I can easily envisage such a world, and in
many parts of Africa that's the way it is! The guy who plays
the drums is fully believed by all and sundry, under the
direction of the powers that be, to make the crops grow . . .
and he makes the rains come at the right time under the
guidance of the priest. That culture hinges on the fact that
there are certain leaders in the musical life which is part
of the spiritual life of the community and that therefore
it's of prime importance to keep that bloke happy and well-
fed . . . Only an extremely materialistic attitude can fail to see
that there's a great deal of truth in this view.

8

MIKE GIBBS

Mike Gibbs was born and brought up in Rhodesia; he studied music for four and a half years in America (1959–63), and he eventually came to live in London in 1963. Since then he has become one of our most successful composer/bandleaders, and one of the most 'inside' jazz musicians in this country . . . he's much in demand as an arranger and composer, and he's composed the background music for two films, but at the same time he can draw large crowds at the Queen Elizabeth Hall when his band plays concerts there. Weaker talents might be swamped by some of his more mundane writing chores, but Mike Gibbs brings quality to everything he does. He is an extremely aware person and also painstakingly honest which is probably why he is almost as indecisive, almost as reluctant to make any assertions, as Derek Bailey. It's almost as if they feel that the mere act of attempted definition is bound to result in distortion. Certainly, the most fundamental fact about Mike Gibbs is that he likes to keep his options (in music as well as life) open as long as possible, and so leaves all final decisions until the last possible moment.

His first job when he came to England was playing the trombone with the Graham Collier Sextet which he did for about two years. Sometime during that period, I bumped

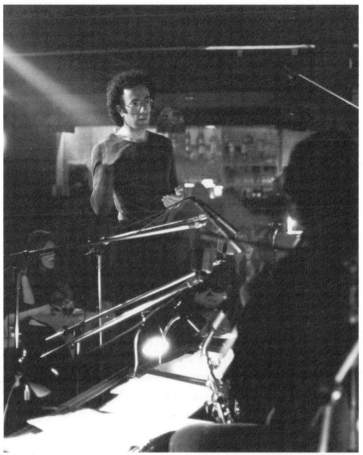

Mike Gibbs (photo Michael Leale)

into him in the centre of London when he was on the horns of a typical dilemma. After agreeing to do a concert with Graham Collier's band, he'd been asked to play with the Tubby Hayes big band on the same day. He'd decided to work with the Hayes band and had booked a deputy trombone player to work with Collier. But then he'd found out that the deputy was the very man whom Mike was replacing in the Tubby Hayes band. So he felt terrible about the whole business. He felt bad about not doing the Collier concert after he'd agreed to do it; he felt bad about taking somebody's place in the Hayes band; he felt doubly bad about adding insult to injury by his unwitting choice of deputy. So, having made his decisions, he still remained in an indecisive state and was on his way to talk to his analyst about the whole thing.

This kind of awkward situation in which Mike Gibbs found himself is of course not at all unusual on the jazz scene. Somebody is always being replaced by somebody else; musicians often put deputies into bands. What is unusual is the extremely sensitive conscience Mike Gibbs displayed. Most musicians build up a tough protective shell, and do what they can to put such disturbing thoughts out of their minds. But Gibbs has achieved the small miracle of refusing to realise his ambitions at the expense of his humanity. Without displaying the kind of ruthlessness our society seems to demand, he has established himself in the last four years or so as being one of the best-known and most respected bandleader/composers on the British scene. And even this has occurred almost despite himself, because he does not seem to initiate things. Instead, things, situations, acclaim, success, seem to happen to him. Even his bandleading began as a sort of happy accident. He explains how it happened:

> In 1968 the BBC asked me to form a band and do a broadcast concert in Lancaster. I formed this band which I didn't intend to keep going, but the concert was so successful that I was then asked to do a broadcast in London. Then I played on a record date with Mike Westbrook and met Peter Eden. John Surman who was in my band suggested to Peter that he record me, and he got me a record contract with Decca . . . By this time the band still didn't seem to be a permanent thing, but I was getting offers of work for it

every few months . . . so the band's kept going ever since without my looking for work for it . . . I've never intended to be sort of a bandleader . . .

But the reluctant bandleader has been winning polls in both the composing and the big band categories. At the same time he makes a very comfortable living because he is a complete professional and a superlative craftsman. His attitude to music is undogmatic, catholic, and practical; all types of music are grist to his mill because for him music is something to enjoy and something to earn a living by. He explains his attitude quite simply:

I can't think of one music as 'commercial' and another as 'my soul' or whatever. It's all a pleasure to me.

So his daily work might include anything from playing the trombone in a studio orchestra (he's an excellent section player, but not a strong soloist), to writing jingles for television commercials or film background music, or working with Bill Oddie on the music for the TV comedy show *The Goodies*, of which he is the musical director. But whether he is involved in this kind of applied music or doing one of the occasional concerts with his own band (pure music), his commitment seems to have an equal intensity. At the same time, his interest in music, his listening habits, and the things which excite or inspire him, cut across all the boundaries and categories and the 'spheres of influence' carved out by journalists and the guardians of traditional culture. Mike Gibbs listens to and learns from 'straight' music, pop, rock, jazz, and anything else that, as he puts it, 'catches his ear'. This liberal and commonsense attitude is all the more remarkable today when we are living in an age of fanatical musical orthodoxies, of almost hysterical compartmentalising which is perpetrated at all levels of society — from the blind partisanship of certain rock or jazz fans, to the cultural caste-system propagated by the BBC which divides all music into two categories: 'serious' and 'entertainment'. The Gibbs outlook obviously comes from the innate character of the man, but it is worthwhile trying to trace the influences which helped to establish it.

His early musical experiences were unexceptional. He began taking piano lessons when he was seven, and also heard the various pop songs of the time on the radio. Eventually, an enlightened piano-teacher introduced him to certain jazz records — Louis Armstrong, Barney Bigard, and Glenn Miller, and his interest developed along the classic lines of the middle and later 1950s: first a liking for the West Coast school of music (Shorty Rogers, Gerry Mulligan, and Dave Brubeck), because this was favoured by the various media and given a lot of exposure; and then the discovery of the East Coast school and Charlie Parker.

When he was about seventeen, Mike Gibbs forsook the piano and began playing trombone. Even this seems to have happened more by chance than design.

> One day at school, I saw a fellow with a saxophone and that appealed to me, so I told him I wanted to learn it. He came back the next day and said that his father, who was also a musician, recommended that I play the trombone. I said, "Well, what's that?" I saw a picture of one somewhere. It was Pee Wee Hunt — Pee Wee Hunt's tune *Oh!.* The sheet music had a picture of him with a trombone on the front and it looked so good! I saved up £17 and bought a brand new trombone and started to learn it.

At that time he was playing with a small group and also writing some arrangements of dance-band tunes for it. They tried to get some bookings playing at dances, but they were also trying to play Dave Brubeck's type of music. After he'd been playing trombone for about four months,

Gibbs left school and went to university. His best subjects at school had been chemistry and physics, so he went to the University of Natal in Pietermaritzburg to study for a science degree. The inevitable happened: he got deeply involved with all the jazz musicians at college (Brubeck's most famous LP was called *Jazz Goes to College*), and failed his second-year exams. But he knew now that he wanted to devote his energies entirely to music, so he wrote to the Berklee School of Music in America and asked for a place there. Then he spent two years doing various jobs in Rhodesia in order to raise the money to get to the USA. Among other things he worked in a laboratory testing soils, and also in a flour mill. But at the same time he carried on playing in the local dance band and also in the Municipal Orchestra which gave him some background in classical music.

The four and a half years of intensive study in America obviously had a tremendous effect on Mike Gibbs. He seems to have derived from this experience not only his conception of what music is all about, but also his general philosophy of life:

In 1959 I went to the Berklee School of Music. It was a four year course, but because they didn't do a degree which for some reason at that time I wanted, students could go to the Boston Conservatory at the same time and do the classical side of music. So I did this, and as I started late it meant that when I'd finished the four years at Berklee I still had another year to go at the Conservatory. At about that time I stopped practising Catholicism and started reading more. I became my own religion in a way. I don't quite know how it has affected the music, but I became much more aware of myself. The strongest teacher for me at Berklee was Herb Pomeroy. Berklee wasn't just a jazz school. They just taught music — commercial music — music you could make a living by — commercial music of which jazz was an extension. So you learned danceband music, music for television, jingle-writing and film writing and one course was in jazz — chord progressions, composition. And the jazz side was organised by Herb Pomeroy. He had a history class and a composing class he taught privately. He ran the big bands and directed what was called the recording band which made a record every year and in which I played for about four years. In the first few summers, to pay for the tuition I worked as an orderly in a hospital. By this time I'd run out of money. I got a few scholarships but they weren't enough to pay for everything, so for the first years the hospital paid my living expenses. Then at the beginning of the third year — 1961, I started working with Herb Pomeroy's big band. Once I'd started working with that I started getting a lot of music work so I could give up the other jobs. I did a lot of jingle playing and band playing, and it kept me going. I also did a lot of copying and paperwork. It paid tuition. It was cheap to live, I just ate cheeseburgers and chocolate milk shakes and scrambled egg!

The way in which Mike Gibbs used these five years in America gives some idea of his total dedication to the task in hand — learning about music. He not only attended the Berklee courses, but also had private tuition, and when the Berklee School was on holiday he would enrol in other courses — in particular, summer schools. This filled out the already broad musical picture for him. In 1961 he went to the Lenox School of Jazz which was run by John Lewis and the Modern Jazz Quartet, and which offered three weeks of music in a holiday setting. Again this had a very strong influence on Gibbs:

J. J. Johnson was there, and I studied with him for a while. And that year, George Russell was there teaching his 'Lydian Chromatic Concept of Tonal Organisation'. This was useful because, although I don't use his Lydian thing, what the concept ends with is a way to play music using any notes. It's just an organised way to be chromatic, so the end result was useful to me. But I found my own way to use the twelve notes chromatically without using his system, so it was good for me from that point of view . . . Dave Baker was also there teaching at Lenox. Gunther Schuller taught the history course there, and after that course I went and studied composition with him privately. He was another important teacher for me. I don't know how influential he was because in the year I studied with him, what he was teaching me was the basics of twelve-tone composition which I don't use now because I was so rigid with the system. I've virtually put aside the things he taught me, but I had to learn them in order to discard them, so it was beneficial from that point of view. But he was very stimulating because he was doing so much. He was very heavily involved in jazz. He's still writing the history of it — the first volume's just come out. At that time he couldn't accept any commissions for the next two or three years because he was so busy. He was just beginning to stop playing the French horn. He was conducting all over the place. This kind of heavy involvement was very exciting . . . it affected me in some way!

It's probably difficult to over-estimate the inspirational value of a teacher like Gunther Schuller. And in a sense, he is a totally un-British phenomenon, because he not only has a deeply instinctive and intellectual understanding of jazz, but he is also equally at home in the world of contemporary (or traditional) non-jazz music. The nearest equivalents in Britain are possibly the composers Don Banks and Richard Rodney Bennett. But the main point about Schuller is that he seems to have a total commitment to both musics — an equal love, understanding, and involvement with both. He taught not only at the Lenox Summer School which was entirely jazz-based, but also at the Tanglewood Summer School which was classically based and the summer home of the Boston Symphony Orchestra.

In his last year in America, 1963, Mike Gibbs went to Tanglewood and spent two intensive months studying and making music:

> The previous year I'd discovered for myself Olivier Messiaen whom I still love and listen to, and Charles Ives. These two composers, I guess, have influenced me a lot. I've based many of my pieces on fragmentary ideas I've got from Messiaen. What I've got from Ives are the sort of multi-layers of music which appealed to me greatly and which I still use a lot today . . . I was very taken with contemporary non-jazz music, although when I look back, it was a more cerebral or intellectual thing that appealed to me. I'd been going to lectures by Pierre Boulez and just the intellect that buzzed around the room when he spoke was very appealing for some reason, although I didn't understand half of it. The music I couldn't understand either, but I think one of its attractions for me lay in the fact that I couldn't understand it. So I applied to go to the Tanglewood Summer School, and I got a scholarship to that. The head of the composition school was Aaron Copland, and we students were very blasé about him. He seemed such an old-fashioned composer to us. I don't think that now, but in those days we hardly noticed what he was doing. Other teachers at the school were Gunther Schuller with whom I'd already been studying, and Yannis Xenakis who was an incredible composer. His music was very emotional and I loved it. Another teacher was Lukas Foss to whose music I could respond emotionally . . . I liked all this intense music but for some reason those two months were very unproductive for me. I couldn't get any pieces of music written in that period, except for the things I was writing for Gary Burton — which had nothing to do with the school anyway.

When the vibraphonist Gary Burton arrived at the Berklee School in 1961 to begin his four-year course, he was already a prodigious soloist with a superb technique and a seemingly inexhaustible flow of ideas. In those days the fashionable tune for jazz ensembles was *On Green Dolphin Street*. Miles Davis had recorded it in 1958 and, as he'd done so many times before and with so many other tunes, he revealed to musicians the emotional depths of the melody and its potential as a vehicle for improvisation. Perhaps it would be more accurate to say that Davis invested the tune with more depth and power than it had ever seemed to have before. John Coltrane did the same sort of thing with the pop song *My Favourite Things*, Coleman Hawkins in the 1930s with *Body and Soul*. Anyway, after the Davis version of *On Green Dolphin Street*, it became one of the most popular themes for jazz musicians. And it was by soloing on this tune that Gary Burton introduced himself to the other musicians at Berklee. So far as Mike Gibbs was concerned — and presumably the other students as well — it was love at first hearing:

> . . . Gary floored everybody! He was already fantastic! He had this incredible technique — he just roared through the chord changes! The harmonies created a bit of a problem for some other players but Gary just roared through it like it was nothing!

It was Gary Burton who was responsible for Gibbs' first serious attempts at composition. Up to this time he'd still thought of himself primarily as a jazz trombonist who also wrote arrangements. When he'd been studying composition he had, of course, written pieces for class projects, but at that time composing didn't come easily to him and he hadn't thought much about doing it. On the other hand he'd done a lot of arranging, and had arranged other people's compositions on the Berklee annual big band recordings. These came out under the blanket title of *Jazz in the Classroom*. In this series, Gibbs had, among other things, arranged half an album of Quincy Jones' tunes. He himself makes this distinction between arranging and composing, but in some cases, for example when the arrangement is very creative or perhaps remoulds the initial material, they must surely have one and the same function. However, his friendship with Gary Burton blossomed into a mutually fruitful musical relationship and when Burton got a record contract with RCA he asked Gibbs to write some music for his first album:

> That's when and how my composing started, and I've been writing for Gary since then . . . he started me composing tunes. Each time he had a record coming up he'd write and ask for material, and I'd write a piece for him. Most of the pieces I've done to date have been for him.

It was also Gary Burton who introduced Mike Gibbs' work to the American saxophonist Stan Getz, and the Gibbs composition *Sweet Rain* became the title-piece of one of Getz's finest albums. As a result of all these gradually proliferating outlets for his talent, when Mike Gibbs eventually came to live in Britain in 1965, he arrived with a pretty strong set of credentials. He had a B.Mus. from the Boston Conservatory and a professional diploma in composing and arranging from Berklee, but, perhaps even more important than these academic qualifications, his talent had already been recognised and accepted by at least two leading American jazz musicians. In the middle 1960s, on the insecure and only partially established British scene, this was an invaluable asset. But even so, it didn't bring automatic acceptance, and it was to take three more years before he began to establish himself here as a composer and bandleader.

In 1963 he'd already made an abortive attempt to settle in London after he'd finished his studies in America:

I had had enough of America. I wanted to do something on my own and I felt that in England I'd be less of an alien. In America I was always an alien and to Americans, although I was Rhodesian, that meant English to them. I felt Rhodesian basically, but thought I'd be more at home in England . . . So I came here in 1963 with the intention of staying, but in the first week I found it so difficult! Looking back, it was only a week, but it was so difficult! I couldn't find a room easily; my money was running out. I think I arrived with about £40 or £50. Nobody seemed to want to know about me, whereas for some reason I thought I was going to make it easily here. I wrote home and my dad suggested I went home to Rhodesia for a few weeks' holiday, but when I got there I found that I couldn't get back to England because there was a two year waiting list for visas and work permits . . . So I thought of going back to America. I had to straighten out my papers because I'd dodged the army in America — legally — but still, they didn't want me back there very quickly. By this time Stan Getz had recorded *Sweet Rain* and Gary and Stan between them got my papers straightened out so that I could go back there . . . and I was on the verge of going back when I met Cilla [his future wife]. She was English so I wanted to stay with her and go back to England again . . . I was in Rhodesia for eighteen months, and again played with the Municipal Orchestra. Also, at that time a young couple there were doing jingle work for the TV which had just opened up. I did all the arranging for their jingles which gave me good experience in studios which I hadn't had apart from a bit of recording in America. Then the army in Rhodesia got on my tail and wanted to call me up. The only way to avoid that, it seemed to me, was to leave . . . I knew I could get work in South Africa, but I was so against the scene there that if I could have saved the money for my passage to

England in Rhodesia, I would have done so — that's what I was aiming at. But the army called me up and I had to avoid that, and the easiest way was to jump into South Africa on a holiday. When I was in South Africa, I got offered work immediately playing in an English ice show that was touring around. So Cilla came down with me and we toured for five months with this company — which was again like a glorious paid holiday. In that five months I earned enough money to come to England, and when the show ended I came back to England with Cilla.

When he was at Berklee, Mike Gibbs had met the British bass player and composer Graham Collier who was also studying there. While Gibbs was in Rhodesia, he corresponded with Collier, and thus ensured a contact in London which proved to be an invaluable help. In fact, no sooner had Mike Gibbs arrived in England than he became a member of Graham Collier's band, which meant that he not only began working immediately but also met many other musicians. He worked with Collier for about two years, and also played with as many rehearsal bands as he could find time for. He also got occasional work such as playing in the orchestra for a pantomime at Wimbledon, and in the pit orchestra for *My Fair Lady* in Norwich, both of which experiences he enjoyed. It was a very different story from his previous disastrous visit. This time, one thing led to another in a gradually escalating series of activities. One of the rehearsal bands he played in was run by the late Tony Russell who was managing John Dankworth's band at the time, and when Cleo Laine needed a trombonist in her accompanying band, Russell recommended Mike Gibbs. He has played with Dankworth's band ever since:

> Working with Dankworth got me a lot of exposure because he asked me to write for the band, and he always gave me a

lot of plugs each time we went somewhere. That got my name about and I started getting session work from then on, so financially, from that period onwards, I was doing OK. And I was still writing for Gary Burton all this time, so my American contacts seemed to keep up!

Then, as mentioned earlier, in 1968 the BBC asked him to form a band for a broadcast, and from that time on he's been leading his own band — and, of course, writing for it. At first he simply arranged pieces that he'd written for other people — Gary Burton in particular, but when the band became a semi-permanent unit, Gibbs began, for the first time in his life, writing things for himself. And he not only began to get more writing commissions, but he also began looking for new contexts in which to compose:

Also in about 1968, I'd been listening to other contemporary non-jazz composers — still Messiaen and Ives, but also Penderecki and Lukas Foss . . . not that many, I guess, and I saw a competition advertised for a composition for a double wind quintet. So I wrote a piece for that . . . for the Portia Wind Ensemble, and it won first prize — £100! They performed it at a prize-winning concert which was a great thrill! . . . Then I'd been playing at the Belfast Festival for a couple of years with the Dankworth band, and Michael Emmerson, the director of the festival, asked me one day what chamber music I liked. I told him that one of my favourite pieces was a Debussy trio sonata for flute, harp and viola. So he asked me to write a piece for that combination. I thought that to write for that combination I would have the Debussy piece in mind too much . . . so I just used those instruments and added oboe and cello which were two instruments I liked a lot . . . That was performed at Belfast, and the following year he asked me to be composer of the year there. Unfortunately, that fell apart because I never got all the music written in time. But the quintet composition was played again, and I also did a concert with Gary Burton

John Dankworth

. . . Then the people at Canterbury asked me to do a concert with my band in the cathedral there. I had just received an Arts Council bursary, so I used the Canterbury concert to play the music I'd written with the bursary. I used the second half of the concert to do that, and the first half was pieces from the repertoire plus a piece that the Canterbury people had commissioned which was called *Canticle*. It's on the *Tanglewood* album and it worked marvellously in the cathedral with the echo . . . I'd been listening to Messiaen's *Turangalila Symphony* which is a long piece in fourteen movements, and one movement of it had such a relaxing effect and made me turn my mind inwards. The feeling it gave was not just pleasant, but it appealed to me so much that I wanted to write a piece of music which would evoke a similar response from me and hopefully from the audience. This is what I tried to achieve in *Canticle* . . . to evoke a certain kind of feeling so that the listener would turn inwards on himself. As it happened, at the concert one of the deans came and said he had liked the piece a lot and that it had had a spiritual effect on him . . . which meant that I had at least partly achieved what I had wanted to.

Eventually Mike Gibbs established the distinctive sound of his own band which included brass, reeds, sometimes

strings, usually an electric keyboard and a guitar, bass guitar, drums and percussion. The resulting music features
multi-layers of sound, sumptuous harmonies, rhythms of
rock and jazz, and several virtuoso soloists. And whatever
his academic qualifications and background, just because
the jazz conception of music has always been central to
his thinking, his development as a composer has been
deeply influenced by the improvising musicians with
whom he has worked. They too are composers, of course,
and it would be true to say that the Gibbs band, like any
really vital jazz group, is made up entirely of composers —
musicians who create the music within forms dreamed up
and established by the band leader. And it is also obvious
that the musicians themselves can affect or alter or create
some of the forms of the music, as well as providing it with
their own flavour and colour. One of the main differences
between jazz and non-jazz Western music to date is that
the jazz musician doesn't see a piece of music as something
fixed and static, but as something which evolves dynamical-
ly and which is always subject to spontaneous change and
growth. And as his composing has developed, Mike Gibbs
has more and more adopted the approach of the improvising jazz musician in his conception of performance:

> When I was at Berklee, I was writing arrangements of tunes
> and each section was very clear. Also in those days, I would
> put a lot of hard work into an arrangement, and when it was
> finished I would never change it. If there was anything wrong
> with it, I would just realise that and benefit from it in a future
> arrangement. But now, the first performances of pieces are
> something I've thrown together the night before, and the
> piece evolves from performance to performance, and as we
> don't do many concerts it takes a long time for a piece to
> evolve. I can't work any other way. I can't go into the first
> performance with a definitive arrangement . . . And I find
> now when I have a project, that I can think about it and work

on it, but I can't actually put it on paper which is like putting a full stop to it, until the last minute . . . At the moment, one of the things I have to do is write a ballet score, and I imagine what will happen, judging from what's happened in the past, and in order to get the greatest amount of spontaneity, is this: I've got a vague idea about the form. I'll start getting musical ideas for it but I won't write them down until the last minute. Whatever ideas I get in the next week or so, while they are lying in my mind they'll have a chance to evolve, and theoretically, if I was to leave them there for ever, they would continue to evolve as long as the project interested me. But however much they have evolved by the deadline, I'll put that down. I can't have a score finished two weeks beforehand because it's incredibly difficult to put anything down — to make that decision.

And as the problems of writing, composing, and band leading become more and more absorbing, Gibbs' trombone playing seems to become less important to him — more a matter of light relief than of central interest:

What playing I do is physical. There's no creativity in it. It's technical and physical. My chops aren't good but I enjoy it. Recently I did two weeks at the Ronnie Scott Club with John Dankworth immediately after doing two weeks there with my own band. I hardly played a note with my band, and then I did two weeks hard playing with John's band and I really enjoyed it! I didn't have the responsibility of keeping the music together. I just sat in the section and declined, with difficulty, playing any solos, which terrify me because that means starting to create in an area I'm not familiar with. I just enjoyed the physicalness of playing, the discipline it required to play a note in the right place and it's totally different for me from writing or composing music. I know that for a lot of people I work with, to play and to create are the same thing. But for me they aren't, unfortunately. At one stage I did want to be a jazz trombone player, but I've no inclination in that direction any more.

What has happened is that his band has become his instrument — his total means of self-expression — and this means that his relationship with the musicians is a very subtle and finely wrought affair. Mike Gibbs is not just pre-determining structures, but also utilising the improvising talents of the players and so has to be involved in the free-wheeling and fluid areas they create. At the same time he has to flavour whatever is happening with his own essence. This means maintaining some sort of control in the freer passages of improvisation which are bound to occur in this sort of set-up. A great deal has been talked during the last decade about 'free' jazz, and there has to be some sort of balance between the freedom of the individual and the collective identity of the band:

> If I'm writing music for musicians, I am using them. If I just say to them, "Play totally freely!" then it can have nothing to do with me. I can't function that way . . . And even total freedom isn't either total or free! It is a kind of framework. Not to have a framework is in itself a framework. Musicians who play thinking they are free can't help but use something they know. If they constantly try to get away from what they know, it's still a kind of framework. I don't know what total freedom means!

So he retains some control over passages of pure improvisation, and if he feels such a section has outlived its usefulness he usually terminates it simply by telling the drummer, John Marshall, to stop playing. But to have this kind of control, his relationship with the musicians has to be based on mutual respect and understanding. And there's no doubt that a very alive interplay exists between him and the musicians. He explains the way it works:

I still leave a lot of room for soloists. I sometimes use the room to colour the music, but sometimes it's not just that — it's not me at all! There's one piece we've just done. It almost seems to me now to be my piece, but when we started, I went to the rehearsal with only two minutes of music written, and now I have a ten-minute piece out of it! We had the band play the little bit I'd written, and then I waited to see what I felt should happen next, and because of the tension that had built up in the bit I'd written, I needed a release of some kind. I felt I could get the release by just having [Alan] Skidmore play a fast freewheeling solo. His kind of playing, which I'm very familiar with, would give me that kind of release. So now we play the written bit and then Skidmore and the rhythm section play very fast, very freely, with a suggestion of fast tempo but not necessarily sticking to a strict 1-2-3-4, and the piece has stayed that way. But really, from the point of view of Skid's solo, I don't know that it belongs to me!

Apart from having multi-layers of sound, the Mike Gibbs band also functions at several musical levels. His conception, true to the general musical developments of the 1960s, is essentially pluralistic. Influences from 'straight' music, commercial music and jazz, are fused together in a fashion which must be bewildering to people who see music in terms of purist pigeonholes:

Whenever an article or review is done on the band, it's always mentioned that the music has a pop flavour — for want of a better word. Then I might be asked what pop music I listen to that this influence should be there. And I don't have specific answers to that question. I do listen to pop music, but not that much. A few years ago, when I became musical director of *The Goodies*, I listened to Crosby, Stills and Nash, and I enjoyed them a lot, but one of the reasons why I listened to them was because I was studying the kind of harmonies they were using because I specifically wanted to use that for the *Goodies* thing. I listened to The Band for the same reasons, but listening to it for commercial reasons, I also enjoyed it!

But as well as the catchy tunefulness and the rhythms of rock or pop, the Gibbs band also features long sections of difficult writing, and the powerful statements of the soloists. And at the same time, the Gibbs talent is working itself out in other much less obvious areas:

> When I was at Berklee a lot of the music teaching was very vertical in its thinking — I learnt chords and I had to read up and down in each beat or half-beat to see whether this note fitted that chord, etc. But now I'm trying to turn the music on its end and make it horizontal because I gradually began to realise that I could have, say, a chord in the left hand at a certain point, and the note directly above it could really belong to the previous chord, and there would be no clash because one's ear can easily relate the note at the top to a previous chord and also be aware of the new chord underneath. It's just like bending time a bit — and bending time has been an important thing to me since then. Carla Bley has achieved this in many of her pieces.

Mike Gibbs somehow manages to have the best of both worlds — the appreciation and acclaim of the cognoscenti, and the kind of income afforded by purely commercial music; *succès d'estime*, and *succès de finance*. He occasionally mutters in disbelief: "My life's one long holiday!" This is because he's paid to do things which he finds continually interesting and fulfilling. Perhaps he deserves it. One musician's wry comment on his success was: "It couldn't have happened to a nicer feller!"

9

IAN CARR
Nucleus

In the spring of 1969 I was deeply miserable. The quintet I'd been co-leading for some five years with Don Rendell (which included Michael Garrick on piano, Dave Green, bass, and Trevor Tomkins, drums) seemed to have gone tired on us. We had been together too long and felt very stale — to my disaffected eye and ear, our music seemed to have become safe, predictable, hopelessly polite.

A few months previously we had met the African percussionist Guy Warren when we worked with him on one of his own LPs, and the experience had been a very stimulating one. He played everything from talking drums to maraccas, cowbells, Indian bells, gourd, bamboo flute, harmonica and tambourine — but more than his music, his attitude to music, his dress, his uninhibited manner seemed to epitomise a completely and refreshingly opposite approach to jazz. The Rendell–Carr Quintet wore dark suits and primly knotted ties and could have merged anonymously into almost any respectable background; our clothes seemed to symbolise the conservatism and safety of our music. But Guy never wore Western clothes. His shaven head would be covered by a black fez or else a kind of straw pith-helmet; over a white African gown he sometimes wore a black cape, sometimes a leopard skin. And he always wore dark glasses.

Though his appearance was wildly exotic, he kept a kind of immensely cool reserve and gave me an almost sinister impression of controlled power. It took some time to discover that behind the awe-inspiring exterior was an extremely sensitive and friendly person. He was then forty-five; after growing up in Ghana, and working for a while in England, he had spent several years in America and had associated with some of the most famous jazz musicians, Charlie Parker one of them. I suddenly thought that perhaps he could give the quintet a new lease of life, and after I discussed the idea with Don Rendell, Guy Warren joined the band.

Although in private he tended to be very gentle and withdrawn, once he appeared on stage with us he was entirely unpredictable; he would move around freely, playing whichever of his instruments he felt appropriate, and would shout out remarks and exhortations — "God save

The Don Rendell–Ian Carr Quintet, 1960s: *Left to right*: Rendell, Dave Green, Mike Garrick, Carr, Trevor Tomkins.

the Queen!" "Motherfucker!" — and over Dave Green's bass solos, in the attentive silence, "Take it slowly, she's only sixteeeeeeen!" Towards the end of the solo he would blow a sort of siren note on his harmonica and shout "Better make it fast! The police are coming!" At a concert at York University, duetting with Don Rendell on the bamboo flute, he became so carried away that he lay on his back on the floor and waggled his pointed slippers at the ceilings — blowing mightily all the while. His whole performance was a kick in the teeth for the traditional and hip idea of the cool improvising genius. Under this sort of assault, the reserve, the Britishness of the group, had to crumble and either shatter into embarrassed fragments or with luck metamorphose into something else.

Apart from the fire and the sheer open-spiritedness that Guy brought to the Quintet, he also brought sound colours and a sense of rhythm quite new to us. Unlike the conventional jazz pulse which tended to put the emphasis on the offbeat (the second and fourth beats in a 4/4 bar), Guy concentrated on the African style, stressing the first and third beats, which produced a surging, rolling and very physical rhythm. He also liked extreme dynamics, his pianissimo flirting with silence while his fortissimo was an orgy of unrestrained volume. These extremes suggested a kind of vitality and reality sadly lacking in the Quintet's own music. But Guy's rich ingredients didn't mix easily with ours. For him a concert was a total experience, visual, theatrical, social, as well as musical — an experience involving the audience as much as the musicians — and the Quintet couldn't absorb his kind of atmosphere and was embarrassed by his theatricality. Nor would he tone down his performance to the polite middle-class level we required. In retrospect, our relationship with him seems absolutely fascinating — a real confrontation of two cultures with each

side too worried about losing its identity to adapt itself to
the other. At the time the dilemma didn't, of course, seem
so clear-cut. After two or three months of collaboration I
had in the end to go along to Guy's flat one afternoon and
explain that the experiment had failed — something he was
in any case well aware of himself.

The contact with Guy Warren gave me experience of a
different culture which opened up new perspectives to me.
In one of his rare moments of confidence he described
how he had travelled all over Ghana with a tape-recorder
recording the indigenous music of the country. And even
in this, he was an isolated and lonely figure. He once
admitted: "Of course, I feel like a stranger in my own
country. The people are mostly stupid and have a high
regard for the white man's principles and values. They
want to *become* like the white man! They scorn their own
African music . . . they are *ashamed* of it! . . . and they try
to get an interest in Western pop music and classical
music. They even try to dress like the white man, and
to *copy* his mannerisms — his stiff politeness and his self-
control!"

Strangely, Guy's attitudes to the royal family had the
ambivalence of the man caught between societies . . . He
seemed to dislike them intensely, but he read avidly everything about them he could get hold of. When the investi-
ture of Prince Charles was shown on television, there can
have been no more attentive observer than Guy. And from
the meticulous care with which he described what he had
seen, it seemed that in reality he loved the royal family. He
certainly had little love or respect for the colonising
English. In moments of stress he would groan: "Oh, if only
I could be a *dog* in England, that's what I'd really like . . .
Yes . . . if you want to be loved and looked after, then you
should be a *dog* in England!"

Guy has no artificial mental barriers about and would never offer a generic condemnation of any kind of music. He has no irrational sense of purity. In Ghana he had played with the Ghana police band in an Africanised performance of Beethoven's *Fifth*. In London, he induced the Rendell–Carr Quintet to record a small group version of Ravel's *Bolero*. Guy played the conventional drumkit for it, and his rolling rhythms were extremely appropriate to the music . . . Ravel would certainly have approved.

The evening after I had ended our association with Guy, I told Don Rendell that I myself was going to leave the Quintet. I had no plans, no idea what I was going to do, or whether I was even going to stay in music. So far as impetus and direction were concerned, I was at an all-time low. That was in July, 1969. By then, a few musicians (Graham Collier, Mike Gibbs, Keith Tippett) had received grants from the Arts Council, so I applied for a grant to write and perform a work for a double quintet. Then I spent the rest of the summer doing any kind of musical work I could get, and teaching at the Barry Summer School jazz course.

It was a period of intense thought and self-examination. Several fundamental questions had to be considered. First, why continue in music at all? I had a degree in literature and some other useful talents, and I was certainly sick of the scrappy and precarious life. But it seemed that the pain of the life-style didn't outweigh the pleasure of it . . . though they seemed to be pretty equally balanced at the time. I was depressed, but I knew from experience that depression lifted, and could still imagine dimly what it would be like when I emerged on the other side. Then I had the feeling that my period with the Quintet had been an apprenticeship – a preparation for something else, and that I had barely scratched the surface of my own potential.

By the end of August I'd come to realise that I was going to carry on as a musician, and that raised the questions, "How?" and "In what capacity?" Why shouldn't I function as a freelance musician — a sideman in other people's bands? I had enjoyed much of the work I'd done for other people — but then I'd always had the Quintet as the focal point of my musical life. I couldn't exist without this kind of centre, and I didn't think I could bring myself to identify totally with someone else's concept if that was to be my only musical diet.

Then I realised that I received fulfilment from having a regular group which worked out its problems collectively. It occurred to me as it had to Jon Hiseman that Americans had been superior in the music, not because they had some innate and magical superiority (the traditional, romantic view), but rather because the cultural and economic climate in America made it possible to keep together regularly working units. This didn't, of course, explain away the individual genius of men like Louis Armstrong, Duke Ellington, Miles Davis or John Coltrane; but in order to flourish, their talents had needed the right climate and the context of regular groups and bands. So I decided that I would start another band.

This involved a whole series of further considerations. I didn't know exactly what kind of band or what kind of music I wanted. At this stage, I knew only what I didn't want, and these negative considerations fell broadly into two categories: organisational and musical. First of all, I was finished with amateurism. In the Rendell—Carr Quintet we had done all our own managing, our own fixing of work, our own promotion, and because we were amateurs at this side of things, and because we had neither the time nor the money to do any really useful promotion, the Quintet had remained a very minor cult. This had

meant that I had had to supplement my earnings by working as a part-time teacher which had devoured too much of
my energy and seriously slowed up my development as a
musician. If I was going to continue in music, I wanted to
be free to devote all my energies to the music itself. It was
essential to find some sort of organisation which would
take care of promotion and find work for the group. And
the idea of 'image' was strongly connected with this
approach.

During the 1960s, the media had made society increasingly image-conscious; the hype merchants had seized on
this and exploited it ruthlessly. One of the main things
which limited the earning power, activities, development
and freedom of the jazz musician was the staleness and the
haphazard nature of his image. Having to compensate
psychologically for their poverty and obscurity, musicians
tended to make a fetish of their lack of work. If one was
ignored, then that was proof of one's quality . . . one was
simply too talented and intelligent to be understood or
appreciated by the general public. Although I'd done my
share of this kind of thinking, it became more and more
apparent that it was an easy way out — a superficial and
facile reaction to a deeply complex situation.

Another disturbing fact was that most young jazz musicians were desperate to play for any fee or for nothing, and
under almost any conditions. Even if they do not naturally
subscribe to this sort of attitude, the traditional image of
the jazz musician — the romantic idea of the improvising
genius bursting to 'say something' — pressurises them to it.
Therefore there is a long tradition of jazz musicians whose
talents, however remarkable, can be bought cheaply — it is
even a point of honour among many of them to be naïve
and incompetent in business affairs, as if this proved the
worth of their creative inspiration. But the exploitation of

this attitude had become more and more evident during the sixties. Universities and colleges, the staple audience for jazz and rock groups, were prepared to pay exorbitant fees for rock musicians while they still kept up the tradition of getting jazz groups on the cheap. A name jazz group booked by a college jazz society might be lucky to get £100 for a concert; but a pop or rock group, booked by the Students' Union Entertainment Committee, might get anything from £200 to £2000. To my way of thinking, in the summer of 1969, the whole jazz world seemed to be riddled with romance — the romance of the inspired, misunderstood genius; the romance of drugs; the romance of the avant-garde. It also seemed that a bit of realism was overdue.

The jazz image was too deeply established to be easily changed, so the first thing in forming a band was to try and avoid the crippling label 'jazz' or at least to reduce its importance. This, apart from the sheer boredom of travelling old territory, was the main reason why I decided not to call the new group the Ian Carr Quintet, but chose the impersonal title Nucleus.

Then there were certain physical aspects to the general organisation that needed changing. The Rendell–Carr Quintet had always used the house public address system wherever it was playing. Sometimes there had been no such facilities at all; more often than not, the quality of the equipment had been very poor. We had to rely on house pianos, and on one or two traumatic occasions there had not even been a piano, so we had been obliged to function as a quartet. Also, a poor piano could utterly destroy the total sound of the Quintet — and the general state of pianos in Britain is absolutely atrocious. So the most important thing from the point of view of physical organisation was never again to be at the mercy of house PAs and house pianos. Somehow we would have to carry around our own amplification. It was also essential either to amplify the double bass adequately, or to use bass guitar . . . I was tired of the imbalance of the traditional sounding group — the dominance of drums and the inaudibility of the 'upright' double bass. At this stage, my idea of the use of electricity was largely as an agent for amplifying the sounds of acoustic instruments. The fact that it might be a rich source of new musical sounds in its own right hadn't yet occurred to me.

As for the music, first of all, I wanted to abandon the old jazz formula: theme/solos all round/theme again. It didn't interest me any more, and I felt that the whole idea of structure and the relationship of written or predetermined passages with improvised passages needed drastic rethinking. Instead of seeing an hour-long set as a series of unrelated, self-contained events, it seemed more sensible to treat it as a single event and try to give it some kind of total shape. But given this broad format, what was going to be put into this hour? What territory was going to be created and explored? There seemed to be two possible approaches: *exclusion* — excluding everything except certain predetermined ingredients; and *inclusion* — selecting all kinds of areas to explore, without any dogmatic or doctrinal rejection of anything. Both approaches are of course equally valid, and they rely for their efficacy or relevance on the temperament and aims of the musician who chooses one or the other.

Throughout my period with the Rendell—Carr Quintet, I had experimented with other musicians in attempts to expand my musical language. Looking back at the history of jazz, I found a definite pattern of development emerging. During the 1930s, jazz had gradually become a more self-conscious art (the obvious example is Duke Ellington);

in the 1940s there were some wilful experimenters (Parker, Gillespie, Monk, etc.), but once they had worked out a new language, a new style, they'd stayed with it and continued to function from within it. Then, during the 1950s and '60s, an even more self-conscious avant-garde grew into a movement that saw honour only in permanent change. It was now no longer enough to break new ground and then spend the rest of the time working out that territory as the beboppers had done. The impetus now was to carry on changing as fundamentally as possible at all costs (which can be seen in the astonishing progress of John Coltrane from 1955 until his death at the age of forty-one in 1967), and to see everything in terms, not so much of good or poor quality, but of progress or non-progress.

This kind of gradual cultural development over the decades is mirrored in the microcosm of each individual jazz musician's development, and the microcosm deserves some examination. In my own case, how had I developed?

What had brought me to jazz in the first place? While at school I had been intoxicated with the whole jazz idea — not just the marvellous sounds and rhythms, but also the apparently exciting lifestyles, the whole image of the jazzman, at that time inseparable from the music. (The school itself — and the music master — were of course very hostile to the idea of jazz, but there was one marvellously sympathetic English master who introduced us to many aspects of twentieth-century art including jazz). I fell in love with the twenties and thirties and early forties sounds and images — the two-toned shoes, the navy-blue shirts and loud ties, the striped shirts and braces, the homburg hats, the double-breasted suits . . . the whole gangster sartorial regalia. And at the same time, the sheer romance of tough, hard-bitten men with cigarettes hanging out of the corners of their mouths and mugs of liquor at hand, all nonchalantly capable of improvising chorus after chorus of beautifully constructed phrases, was an extremely seductive vision. It gave me a vision of a duality which I still find irresistible to this day — rough, tough, wisecracking and laconic men of the world who at the same time have other-worldly gifts, artistic imagination, emotional depth; and in a way, it redressed the balance of my early education which tended to put art and the artist on an absurdly high pedestal . . . as if to be worshipped from a reverent distance.

This initial infatuation progressed to a more thorough examination of the music. At first, the initial emotional impulse is still whole — the sheer joy in playing, the excitement of self-expression, the delight of rhythm, the ease of identifying with the image. But after a while, a few things begin to get in the way . . . logistics, lack of work, personality problems in the group, etc. Difficulties engender self-consciousness: the whole situation has to be re-appraised, and the whole basic philosophy to be re-examined. This analytic habit carries over to the music itself, and soon the natural and unselfconscious emotional involvement in what you are doing becomes encumbered by philosophical thoughts about what you think you ought to be doing. Once some perspective of the music's historical development is acquired, the musician begins to see himself as part of that history. It is a small step from here to the realisation that the people who make an impact, the people who are commonly considered to be the most important and memorable, are the trail-blazers, the ones who break new ground. Suddenly, it is no longer enough simply to enjoy playing and to enjoy doing something well. The irresistible urge to be memorable, to leave one's mark, to write one's name on the universal lavatory wall, has become a vital factor in these considerations. The seductive idea of progress, of breaking new ground, becomes an overriding factor. The audience is no longer just that bunch of people sitting in front of the bandstand; it is also the abstract audience of posterity. It becomes imperative to be 'original', and not just within the confines of existing structures, but in trying to create new structures.

At this stage of imagination and awareness, the intellect seems to have some strong power over emotional impetus. It seems that the intellect has to approve of the course or chosen direction of the music before the natural emotional power can be released. And it is at this stage that many musicians either give up altogether, or at least stop allowing their consciousness to explore its potential and settle into well-defined habits of playing. A few try to meet this challenge and this is very much a phenomenon of the last fifteen years or so.

Of course, apart from prestige and the approval of posterity, there is also money to be made if one can establish that one is a true original. The twentieth century is the age of admass, of mass events and therefore mass anonymity, and the admass man, yearning for something personal and unique, will spend his money on anything that purports to be original, or special. In painting, pop music, the theatre, films, and 'straight' music, a reputation for originality or eccentric novelty is a sure-fire selling point. It was, therefore, essential to realise that the idea of progress, like money, success or security, could become just another bitch-goddess, another false trail, another red herring.

In the world apparently gone mad, split into ideological musical camps, and often bickering about who or what was the most original or the most significant, the only sane thing to do seemed to be to say: "To hell with dogma! . . . I'm going to try and rediscover or re-create total emotional commitment to the music, and rely on whatever

Nucleus in the mid–1980s: Dill Katz (bass guitar), Phil Todd (saxes, flute),
John Marshall (drums), Ian Carr (trumpet/flugelhorn), and Mark Wood
(guitar). Photo © Nick White.

feels good, whether it fits with current trends or not." I
certainly did not want to limit myself to playing 'free' jazz
(improvisation without tonalities, harmonies, time signatures or predetermined structures), though the 'free' area
could certainly play an important part in a conception
which included roots, rhythms, time signatures, tonalities,
and harmonies. I was interested in an inclusive, pluralistic
conception.

So I had decided to form Nucleus. The first thing to do
was to decide which musicians to ask to join it. Three or
four years previously, I'd been one of the judges of the
semi-final of the inter-university jazz competition. (After
the almost total capitulation of universities and colleges to
rock music, jazz competitions were abandoned — in fact,

the one I was judging was probably the last.) The semi-final was held at Sussex University, and the band we voted into first place and later won the final was led by Karl Jenkins. We were really impressed by the spirit of the band, the musicianship, and by Karl's compositions.

After getting a degree in music at Cardiff University, Karl had spent two weeks at the Barry Summer School jazz course, and then come to London to join Graham Collier's band. In the summer of 1968 we did a few after-noon rehearsals at the Troubadour Club, playing Karl's tunes. John Marshall, also a mainstay of the Graham Collier band, was on drums for these rehearsals. Again, I was impressed by Karl's writing and also pleased that he had asked me to go along and play for him. He also seemed interested in the kind of musical areas which appealed to me. He himself plays oboe, baritone and elec-tric piano.

By the following summer (1969), he had left Graham Collier and didn't seem to be doing anything in particular, so I asked him round for a chat. It was the first real and lengthy conversation I'd had with him. He had been and still was deeply depressed by the death of his father the previous year, and was ready for a fresh start. I asked him how he felt about joining me in forming a band which would explore elements of rock music as well as the usual jazz areas. Karl was interested, so we discussed whom we should ask to join us.

John Marshall was the obvious choice on drums. He had developed in both the jazz and rock traditions, and Karl had been associated with him for some time in the Collier band. He had also deputised for Trevor Tomkins with the Rendell–Carr Quintet on several occasions and these experiences had always been musically very happy. Jeff Clyne was also the obvious choice on bass. A master bass player, with an open mind, he had recently taken up the bass guitar. We discussed various saxophonists, but I eventually asked Brian Smith to join us because I'd played with him both in Alexis Korner's band and with John Stevens at the Little Theatre Club, and knew that his conception was a very total one . . . he was at home with anything from 'free' jazz to chord sequences, rock rhythms and the blues. We had some trouble finding a guitarist, but eventually someone recommended Bernie Holland, a young guitarist from the rock scene, and he was with us until the end of 1969.

Having more or less decided whom to ask to join the group, I began to feel that dry prickle of excitement again — a marvellous feeling of buoyancy and hope. Determined to involve myself in a music that meant something to me at the deepest possible level (because I knew that only in this way could I gather enough excitement to give myself unstoppable momentum), I sat down and wrote a list of all the musical influences that had formed me, and all the things I loved very deeply. I tried to make this list as honest and comprehensive as neurosis and memory would allow. I've kept this list and the comments I wrote on it:

> Fats Waller, Lionel Hampton, Benny Goodman, Mel Powell with the AEF band playing *My Guy's Come Back* on the radio during the war.
> Looming very large: Mezzrow–Ladnier Quintet with Teddy Bunn's vocal on the blues *If You See Me Coming*.
> Boogie-woogie . . . Pinetop Smith, Meade Lux Lewis, Jimmy Yancey, Albert Ammons, Pete Johnson.
> Little Richard, Louis Jordan and the Timpani Five.
> Muggsy Spanier — *Relaxin' at Touro, That Da Da Strain*.
> King Oliver's *Snag It.* All Louis Armstrong, and in particular, *Potato Head Blues, West End Blues, Blues in the South, Blues for Yesterday, Back o' Town Blues*.

Bessie Smith . . . *St. Louis Blues* (with Louis of course),
Nobody Knows You When You're Down and Out.
Bix Beiderbecke, Bunk Johnson's *Tishomingo Blues, One
Sweet Letter from You.*
Particularly deep and powerful, the memory of early
experience of the blues — vocal and instrumental . . . goose-
flesh and spine-tingling — and gospels and worksongs
. . . Lightnin' Hopkins, Leadbelly, Joe Turner, Ray Charles,
Sister Rosetta Tharpe and Mary Knight.
Jelly Roll Morton . . . one of my all-time favourites! . . . *Dr.
Jazz, Steamboat Stomp, Cannonball Blues, Whinin' Boy, I
Thought I Heard Buddy Bolden Say, 219 Blues.*
Duke Ellington . . . *Mood Indigo, Black and Tan Fantasy,
Creole Love Call.*
Charlie Parker, Dizzy Gillespie, Thelonious Monk, Art
Blakey, Horace Silver, Miles Davis, John Coltrane.
Other considerations — the fruitful collaborations with gui-
tarist Amancio D'Silva and Guy Warren . . . the one from
India, the other from Africa.
But the biggest single factor is the blues.

It did me good, writing out that list. It reminded me
where I'd come from, and provided ballast for the next
voyage. Also, it was a reminder that, in this sometimes
inhospitable world, one wasn't alone; one was in good
company. It was impossible to go back, of course, but, at
the same time, I wasn't interested in any kind of progress
which attempted to ignore all these roots.

Pete King, the manager of the Ronnie Scott Club, rang
me up. He'd heard I was starting a new band and he wanted to put it on at the club. This was welcome news. The
Rendell—Carr Quintet had played at the Scott Club on
only about three occasions. Three nights in five years!
They couldn't have liked us very much. I went down to the
club to talk to Pete King about it. He seemed extremely
enthusiastic about Nucleus. "Now look here, Ian," he said

earnestly, "I've got an arrangement with a record company and I'd like to record you!" This was interesting. I was beginning to feel desired, wanted, sought after — for a British jazz musician a unique and intoxicating experience. "But I'm still under contract to record with Denis Preston," I said. Pete squeezed my knee. "We can do something about that," he said, tears of joy in the corners of his eyes. "Listen, I've got a good deal . . . don't waste this band!" Then he punched me in the belly and ruffled my hair. I began to feel that he really liked me.

Out of the five Rendell–Carr LPs, over five and a half years I'd made a grand total of about £200 from royalties. There was no survival value in perpetuating the existing arrangements. I went along with Pete King to talk to Denis Preston. Denis said he would free me from my existing contract for a half per cent interest in my new contract and Pete King agreed to this. Later Denis gave me some father-ly advice: "Now you must make sure that you take some extra money as bandleader. You could at least do the sim-ple thing of dividing everything by seven and taking two portions for yourself . . . that's what Chris Barber does." But he gave me no advice about what to look for in my new recording contract.

The rest of 1969 was spent in tying up loose ends, severing the connections with the old way of life and estab-lishing the patterns of the new. During that period, I spent a week in Amsterdam playing with a European Broadcasting Union orchestra which drew its musicians from several countries. I also made a final LP for Denis Preston when we recorded Neil Ardley's *Greek Variations*, and took part in a concert of the late Mike Taylor's music at the London School of Economics. The Arts Council agreed to give me a grant to write something for a double quintet, and sent me half of the money in December. Thus encouraged, I handed in my notice as a part-time teacher and by Christmas was, for the first time in my life, a fully professional musician.

At the beginning of 1970, Bernie Holland opted out, preferring to return to the rock scene, and Chris Spedding joined Nucleus in his place, and for about fifteen months after this the personnel remained stable. The first few months of 1970 were extremely exciting, and also something of a psychological strain. As mentioned in the chapter on Mike Westbrook, one of the characteristics of the jazz scene at that time was its deep conservatism, its tribal conformity, and its extreme suspicion about anything that did not easily fit in to existing thought or behaviour patterns. Nucleus had simultaneously broken several taboos. First, there was the impersonal, un-jazz name. Then, we were as electronic as possible, with electric guitar, piano and bass, and a PA system for the horns. There was much muttering about the purity of acoustic instruments, and the unmusical thing we were doing. And finally, we were exploring the ostinato bass patterns of rock music. During the 1960s, the jazz scene had an almost medieval hatred and dread of rock or pop music. There was a very widespread feeling that, in an almost religious sense, one could be tainted by contact with rock music. This whole attitude seemed to spring from a residue of dogged, provincial puritanism. The sensual pleasure of rock rhythm which Nucleus has always revelled in, was anathema to the sackcloth-and-ashes approach of more self-conscious experimenters.

The general atmosphere of disapproval didn't worry me personally very much. The Rendell–Carr Quintet had always been outside of the 'hip' scene which, until the end of the 1960s, really meant either the Ronnie Scott Club, or the Old Place. But it did upset some of the other members of Nucleus. We recorded our first album in January, and I think it was the lack of confidence generally, and the awareness of certain external psychological pressure which made the experience on the whole a rather gloomy one. But even in recording we were beginning to cease to function in the old jazz way. Up to this time, jazz groups had usually simply gone into a studio and played as they would at a 'live' concert. In other words, the recording was an attempt to capture a performance. This approach had been typical of all the Rendell–Carr albums except the final one, *Change Is*, which on the first side makes use of certain studio techniques such as cross-fading, and the editing of pre-recorded material.

Nucleus was still, of course, interested in capturing performances, but we were becoming equally interested in using the medium of the recording studio. This means making a dear distinction between playing a concert and recording an album. At a concert, improvisation would play a very large part in the performance and would to a great degree govern the shape or structure of the music. On the other hand, a recording would be planned beforehand, the amount of improvisation would be controlled, and any appropriate recording device would be used to contribute to the overall interest of the album . . . over-dubbing, cross-fading, and detailed editing and control of the final tapes. *Elastic Rock* involved all of these techniques.

In the early months of 1970, John Peel and his producer John Walters heard Nucleus, liked the group, and offered it a broadcast on Peel's *Top Gear* show, at that time the most popular show on Radio One. Our appearance on that programme made a huge number of people aware of the existence of Nucleus. Also then, the BBC chose Nucleus to represent Great Britain at the International Jazz Festival at Montreux in June. Although

this was an unpaid honour, it meant the possibility of exposure to a wide Continental audience as the competition
involved groups from about sixteen different countries,
and the whole thing was recorded and televised. This part
of the Montreux festival was an event sponsored by the
EBU (European Broadcasting Union), which ensured that
the tapes and films of the competition were given the
widest possible international distribution. Needless to say,
the musicians representing other countries were not
expected to give their services gratis, and were all paid by
the radio stations which had sent them to Montreux.

I didn't, of course, believe in artistic competitions at anything above the executive — craftsmanship — level e.g. brass
bands and symphony orchestras, both of which set out to
interpret commonly available written music as a basis on
which some judgement could be made. But a performance
by a jazz group, in which the executive musicians were the
composers in action . . . that was surely an impossible task
from an aesthetic point of view, and an exercise in futility.
Above a certain level of competence, there are only different conceptions and different approaches in jazz. In other
words, there's no top or bottom of the league. However,
despite my non-belief, if Nucleus had to compete in order
to go to Montreux, then compete we would. Equally from
the start I had no belief in winning, because such judge-
ments usually rely on the state of mind of the judges, the
kind of values they are used to, and various other uncontrollable factors such as what sort of a bowel movement
they've had on the day of judgement. So far as I was concerned, if the Nucleus set at Montreux pleased me, I
would be well satisfied, whether we won or not. I felt in any
case that the panel of critics would have an inbuilt prejudice against the kind of music we were playing. Events were
to prove me wrong.

My memory of the actual competition is hazy. Earlier in the day we had run through our programme to enable the radio and TV people to get a sound-balance ready for the competition proper, and when we finished that run-through, other competing musicians who were sitting in the audience awaiting their turn to play had burst into sponta-neous applause. This surprisingly generous demonstration warmed our hearts. Primed with this sort of reception from our peers, we were sure to enjoy playing, whatever hap-pened afterwards. In fact, all I remember of the event is that the group seemed to play with tremendous fire, and John Marshall didn't throw one of his monumental depres-sions which used to turn him into a moustache and a pair of glasses poised over a right hand which went up and down nervelessly, a possibility which had been my main worry. He'd done it twice previously — once in the record-ing studio when we were making *Elastic Rock*, and once the night before we left England for Montreux — when Germany had knocked England out of the World Cup — and so beyond recall was his spirit on those two occasions that I was unnerved. However, the untoward didn't happen.

The rule of the competition was that each set by a com-peting band had to last twenty minutes, give or take a minute or so. By discreet signals, BBC producer Ray Harvey, who accompanied us to Montreux, kept me informed of the last five-minute count-down, and we fin-ished our set in twenty minutes and twenty seconds. Sometime later that evening we were told that we'd won.

We drove back to Britain in high spirits. Our success had been announced on the national news, and the release of our first album — *Elastic Rock* — was going to coincide with all this publicity. It certainly seemed that everything was happening for the best in the best of all possible worlds, and this euphoric atmosphere was to last for at least another month.

Three weeks after we got back to England, we were in a Jumbo jet heading for the USA. Winning first prize at Montreux meant that we would appear at the Newport Festival. We were the first British jazz group to play at Newport for about ten years, and as it was also my first visit to the States, the whole occasion took on a great deal of significance for me. We spent three days at Newport, playing on the afternoon of the final day, and then spent a couple of days in New York and played a set at the Village Gate. The five days were enough to give me a really intense whiff of the atmosphere of America, and they also enabled me to lay, once and for all, the ghost which has haunted British jazz from the very beginning . . . the alleged crushing superiority of American music. At Newport and in New York we met old friends who had become an integral part of the American scene — John McLaughlin, Rick Laird, Jack Bruce, Dave Holland, and pianist Dave MacRae who was at that time playing with the Buddy Rich orchestra. (Less than a year later, Dave was to join Nucleus in place of Chris Spedding.) American musicians were extremely friendly and also showed a great deal of interest in and curiosity about the kind of music we were playing.

The country itself left an impression of vastness and great extremes . . . a kind of Brobdingnag to Britain's Lilliput . . . the huge distances, the dry heat of the summer, the coldness of the iced drinks, the violence of sudden thunderstorms. The people themselves gave an impression of immense professionalism. Whatever they did, they did it with total commitment, total concentration, and to the exclusion of all irrelevancies. One got the feeling that it was a land where people only had time to eat snacks (hot-dogs, hamburgers, iced Coca-Cola), because they were so busy preparing superb banquets for the consumption of others.

We spent the Friday and Saturday absorbing the atmosphere of the Festival and listening to all the other musicians, groups, and singers. The kind of professionalism we saw everywhere was already a part of the Nucleus thinking. We too had been aspiring towards the condition of total concentration and involvement from the moment we started playing. In other words, the idea of going on stage and slowly warming up until the right intensity and togetherness was achieved was out of the question. All that sort of limbering up and mental preparation had to be done beforehand. Once in front of an audience, you had to be ready to condense the essence of your message into twenty or thirty minutes. Even the famous and popular Cannonball Adderley Quintet had no more than twenty-five minutes or so on stage — and they used every second of their time.

The Nucleus set was the first event on the Sunday afternoon, and it took place before an audience of a few thousand people sitting in brilliant sunshine. Just before we were due to go onstage, the enormity of the occasion began to hit me and my mouth went dry — a condition with a disastrous effect on brass players. I placed my trumpet and flugelhorn on the side of the steps leading to the stage and rushed off to buy a glass of iced Coca-Cola. When I got back, I picked up the instruments only to find that my trumpet was unplayable — one of the valves had stuck because someone had either kicked it or stood on it accidentally as it lay on the steps. This put me in such a vicious temper that my nerves totally disappeared. Also, the other members of Nucleus, appalled by my apparent bad luck, seemed to prepare themselves to make a special effort to compensate for the fact that I had to play flugelhorn for the whole set. The result of my almost uncontrollable rage, and of the corporate will of the other members of the band, was that Nucleus exploded on the Newport audience like a bomb. At the end of our twenty-five minute set we were given a tremendous ovation by audience, other musicians, and various critics.

Rumour has it that old John Hammond, the man who discovered Billie Holiday, was so pleased with our music that he embraced each member of Nucleus. He did not, however, get the chance to embrace me, because I had tottered offstage straight into the metaphorical arms of Leonard Feather. At this point events began to take on the atmosphere of a dream . . . Leonard Feather . . . a chunk of walking history, a legendary figure . . . I possessed his books: *Inside Be-Bop*, *The Book of Jazz*, and of course his *Encyclopedia of Jazz*, and had been using them and studying them for years. It seemed staggering that he should be wanting to interview me, and not vice-versa. After talking to him, I had to go off to an NBC mobile radio unit to be interviewed on the air. (The NBC live coverage of Newport was, incidentally, sponsored by Ultra-Brite toothpaste). Fred Collins, the boss of the network, was a very relaxed and friendly character, which was just as well because the sight of the old-fashioned, brown, upright microphone with 'NBC' stamped in cream letters across its base, again seemed to heighten the dream-like atmosphere, the sense of history, the feeling of déjà vu.

On the Monday we flew to New York and played the set at the Village Gate. Again the reception was very enthusiastic as were the reviews we read afterwards. It seemed that we could do no wrong in America. A day or so later we were once more in a Jumbo jet flying back to London . . . away from the madness, electricity, enthusiasm, friendliness, open-spiritedness, the extremes and the professionalism of America, and back to the quiet anonymity of Britain. It was like returning from a forest full of wild beasts where one could never be certain who was the hunter or who or what was being hunted, to a small landscape garden with some plaster gnomes in it. For two months after our return nothing interesting happened — no press coverage, no work, nothing. The Leonard Feather article appeared in the *Melody Maker* reviewing us at Newport, but generally speaking, as far as the British media were concerned, we did not exist.

The rest of 1970 we spent in playing at one or two festivals on the Continent, doing one or two concerts in England, and recording two more LPs. We recorded the album *We'll Talk About It Later* in September, and the opening track, *Song for the Bearded Lady*, was certainly Karl Jenkins' most brilliant composition to date. Throughout the first year of Nucleus, Karl's compositions were a perpetual inspiration to the band, and the main characteristics of his style reached a new peak of expression in his *Bearded Lady* composition . . . the immensely sophisticated sense of time, the displaced accents, the melodic flair, the superb integration of bass line and melody line, and the masterful control of tension. After three years, I still find this an exciting theme to play.

Three months after that recording session, we went into the studios again with an augmented band and recorded the fruits of my Arts Council award — *Solar Plexus*. I had been brooding on this long composition intermittently for the whole year, and it turned out to be a sort of summary of my musical experience to date, and a pointer to some future development. The problem, as is usual for me, was not what to put in, but what to leave out.

In a band like Nucleus, in which the personalities and the individual talents are so powerful, there are inevitably clashes of ego, 1970 was a year of continual adjustment and readjustment within the group. It was a period of very rapid musical development: from having only a vague idea of our direction in January, we had by December firmly established a very clear musical vision. This progression was very much the result of the interaction of the six musicians.

In John Marshall, we were very lucky to have a drummer who plays and thinks compositionally. In other words, he is always aware of the total sound of a group, and has a thorough understanding of the various processes of building up and releasing tension. Also, John is one of the very few British jazz drummers who really understand rock music and can handle a very slow pulse. When he eventually left the band to join Jack Bruce, what we looked for particularly when trying new drummers was how slowly they could play with comfort. According to the tabla player, Keshav Sathe, a similar criterion is applied in Indian music. He tells the story of a tabla player who went to a 9 a.m. audition with a sitar player who had the reputation for being a bit of a tyrant. The tabla player played one beat on his tabla and said to the sitar player: "You keep playing, and I'll be back at 9 a.m. tomorrow morning to play my second beat!"

During that first year of the group's existence, Chris Spedding had a great impact on the development of the music. He introduced us to an LP which was to have probably the greatest single influence on the basic musical thinking of Nucleus. This was the album *Blues Now* by Howlin' Wolf — and, in particular, the track called *Smokestack Lightning*. This had several ingredients which became part of the Nucleus conception — a three-bar bass-line full of rhythmic and melodic interest, and a very strong structure which involved the dramatic use of wah-wah pedals, fuzz, distortion, layers of sound, and multi-coloured textures. This track's influence is strongly evident in the Nucleus album *We'll Talk About It*

Later, and to varying degrees in subsequent albums.

In order to keep Nucleus together it was essential to get it on a sound economic basis, and I believed that management would achieve this. The trouble is, that once a group gets management, it is in a different league and is subject to heavy competition. After our successful American trip, the inertia in England and the lack of any follow-up began to shake the solidarity of the group. Chris Spedding who was much in demand as a session guitarist in the recording studios was the first to leave. He went in April 1971, and Jeff Clyne opted out at the same time. Their places were taken by Dave MacRae on electric piano and Roy Babbington on bass guitar. In October 1971, John Marshall left to join first Jack Bruce, and then, some months later, the Soft Machine. His departure was a blow because he was in many ways irreplaceable, but Nucleus was not in a financial position to offer anybody anything much at that time. Certainly, John's leaving seemed to upset Karl very much. They have always had a very good musical understanding and had been closely associated for several years. In June 1972, Karl also joined the Soft Machine, and the basic personnel of Nucleus was then myself, Brian Smith, Dave MacRae, Roy Babbington, and either Clive Thacker or Tony Levin on drums, sometimes both.

I find it difficult to write about people who are currently fairly closely associated with me, but I must say something about the two New Zealanders, Brian Smith and Dave MacRae. They are both virtuosi and complete masters of all aspects of improvisation. Brian has been a continual source of inspiration since Nucleus was formed. He is a quiet man of rare quality — the kind of person who is often overlooked in a society like ours which only notices people who shout at the top of their voices. He played in a rock band in New Zealand with Dave MacRae until they both went to Australia where they met up with bassist Rick Laird (currently with John McLaughlin's Mahavishnu Orchestra) and all three of them played together in a well-known Australian rock band called the Bob Parris Combo. Brian came to England in 1964 and played with various bands, including Alexis Korner, other R&B groups, and the Maynard Ferguson big band with which he stayed for about three years, and toured America. This geographically and musically broad experience is reflected in his general outlook, which is tolerant and outgoing.

Dave MacRae has had a similarly wide experience. In Australia he worked as an arranger/producer for a record company turning out half-a-dozen pop singles a week, and he also wrote a jazz ballet which was performed in Melbourne by the American Dance Theatre. In 1969 he went to the USA where he worked for the next two years. He became involved with the Los Angeles community playing mostly with various kinds of experimental bands, and he spent a year on the road with the Buddy Rich Band touring US and European festivals. Rick Laird was the bass player in the band at that time. Dave also played with Duke Ellington and Dizzy Gillespie at the Monterey festival in 1970. He arrived in England in the summer of 1971 and joined Nucleus almost immediately. He brought a new dimension to the band, because he has a thorough understanding of electronics and their use in music. His conception is rooted in the jazz and rock tradition, but it is also devastatingly original.

In July 1972, we recorded the album *Belladonna*. This was our first recording session for eighteen months because management problems had made it impossible for us to record in the interim. Although we had hardly worked for the six months prior to the recording I was well-pleased with the way the eight-piece group functioned as an improvising unit in the studio. It felt and sounded as if the band had been together on a regular basis for months, and one of the tracks, *Suspension*, although it had never been played before by that group and was given a mere five minutes' rehearsal and some verbal directions, turned out to be perhaps the most perfect track, from the point of view of the relationship between what was written and predetermined and what was improvised, that we'd recorded to date. Here again, the collective playing of the group seemed to be of a very high order — though reviewers still kept talking about solos.

At the beginning of 1973, we found a new manager and now at last the organisational basis of the band is gradually being sorted out. This is of crucial importance because it leaves me free to concentrate on the music. Optimism and vision returned and in March I completed a commission for the Park Lane Group. This was called *Labyrinth* and, like *Solar Plexus*, was for an augmented band. *Labyrinth* is much more musically integrated than *Solar Plexus* in the sense that every key change and every harmony, every written passage and every improvised passage, is very closely and systematically related to the initial theme of the piece. Also the role of the three main soloists (Norma Winstone, Kenny Wheeler, and Tony Coe) is clearly and organically developed. After *Solar Plexus* I felt as if I'd finished my apprenticeship and had arrived at a starting point. *Belladonna* and *Labyrinth* are the first fruits of this new stage.

The album *Roots*, recorded in August 1973, is an attempt to explore the link between our contemporary experiments and the common sources of jazz and the rock music which are, of course, the blues, the hot gospels and worksongs. The essence of these three forms is on the *Roots* album.

POSTSCRIPT: THIRTY YEARS ON

Roger Cotterrell

Music Outside is one of the classic books about contemporary jazz. Vividly and sensitively it captures the spirit, optimism and creativity of a particular moment, a certain time and place. If you weren't there to experience it you need the book to know what you missed; if you were, Ian Carr's text conjures up fond memories as well as new insights. The period covered is admittedly limited — the second half of the 1960s and the beginning of the seventies — and *Music Outside* describes developments in just one country, Britain. But, in this case, time and place were crucial and Carr was there, an important part of the action as well as a sharp observer of it. He wrote about his friends and colleagues, his jazz contemporaries, the people who made the jazz world come alive at one of the most exciting times in its recent history.

During the few years this book takes us back to, Britain really was a special place of jazz innovation. In the sixties something happened, not just in jazz but in pop music and in many areas of the arts, to liberate creative ideas and produce a self-confidence that gave Britain a prominent place on the contemporary arts map. In music, new directions were set that would influence developments in many countries in the following years. The blues revolution happened in pop music, producing a new infusion of black music traditions and spontaneity, and early in the sixties the Beatles, the Rolling Stones and others set out to conquer the world. John Lennon ridiculed the jazz scene, portraying it as populated by middle-aged men swigging pints of beer and listening to the same old riffs. Certainly one effect of pop music's vitality was to point up rather sharply how staid much of the modern jazz world was by comparison. But, perhaps as a necessary (and almost immediate) reaction to this wake-up call, great gusts of fresh musical air began to waft in to jazz and continued to do so as the sixties rolled on.

Amongst other things, jazz in Britain began to ally itself with other arts and other music: there was jazz-rock, jazz and folk music, jazz and South African township music, Indo-jazz fusions, jazz and serial composition, jazz and poetry, jazz and dance, jazz and theatre, and so on. Instrumentalists suddenly emerged, as if from nowhere, not playing the time-honoured, dark-suit-and-tie hard bop of Tubby Hayes, Ronnie Scott and their friends. Instead they created looser, often more obviously emotional and sometimes frankly experimental styles that broke many of the previously accepted rules of modern jazz. Sometimes the musical net was cast so wide for inspiration that the label 'jazz' became irksome, at least for a time. For some musicians, the search took them into approaches to improvisation that they saw as a rejection of jazz methods. But almost all the instrumentalists Carr wrote about were clearly jazz musicians, steeped in jazz but determined to make new statements not constrained by tradition.

New jazz composers appeared too, such as Michael Garrick, Mike Gibbs, Graham Collier, Neil Ardley and Mike Westbrook. Even a brief hearing of some of their music suggested something new was in the air. Garrick

Malcolm Griffiths (*left*) and Mike Gibbs.

tried to put something specifically English into his composing. Not unreasonably, he asked why, having grown up in
Enfield, he should need to try to express himself musically like a native of Chicago or New York. But this was a
revolutionary idea when put alongside the assumptions of
the Hayes—Scott school that the aim was to get as close as
possible to the way the American masters did things.

Mike Gibbs drew on rock rhythms, whereas most jazz
musicians of the previous generation had looked on rock
with unconcealed hatred. After all, it was only a few years
previously, in the second half of the fifties, that legions of
twanging guitars, inspired by Elvis Presley and Bill Haley,
had arrived to steal young audiences away from modern
jazz and the harmonically sophisticated forms of popular
music linked to it. But Gibbs and others were not trying to
water down jazz with rock elements to make it saleable.
They used rock idioms because they liked them and
appreciated their power and immediacy. Neil Ardley and
Mike Westbrook gradually chose large-scale forms for

their compositions, also using rock and other influences from beyond jazz. Westbrook sometimes included bits of sentimental old pop songs in among wild collective improvisations in his works, signalling, as clearly as anyone could, that old prejudices were worth throwing on the scrapheap. Collier, perhaps eventually the most radical of all, started on his long quest to rethink completely the role of the composer in jazz.

It was a hugely exciting time. It sometimes seemed that everyone involved in making the new jazz was trying to go their own way, brimming with the confidence of youth and no longer tied into waiting for the next new thing from across the Atlantic. A fresh name was needed. The ferment of activity was labelled *contemporary* jazz, rather than modern jazz, perhaps to distinguish it clearly from the music of the suits-and-ties modernists who still looked to New York for ideas. The prevailing atmosphere was let's try it, and let's try it our way.

A great deal of this atmosphere is captured in Ian Carr's book and — unfortunately perhaps — it is the only book we have that gives a really informed look at this period by someone who was there and central to events. So, for many reasons, its republication is long overdue. Carr makes clear from the opening pages that he has a mission and in places the anger shows through. Jazz — especially in the UK, less so on the Continent — is a 'music outside' unappreciated by the cultural establishment, 'a perpetual Cinderella of the arts'. Looking back now we can ask whether much has changed. The other main theme is the need to escape labels and break down divisions between musical genres. Again, how much is different now? Kenny Wheeler once told me in an interview, "I can't see why there shouldn't be jazz listeners who listen to all jazz. I can't see why it has to be pigeonholed." But jazz fans are still often the enemies of the new or different; a vigilante force to protect their meaning of the word 'jazz'. The new British jazz of the early 1970s certainly found loyal audiences who — especially if they heard the music live regularly in London — could get a sense of the continuous developments going on, and of how idioms were being built in performance. But, as always, it was the musicians who had to take responsibility for following their musical inclinations and hoping that they would attract an audience. Many of them (as some of Carr's interviewees reveal) relied on putting their music first and accepting the breadline existence that went with it — something easier to do while young and energetic, without family responsibilities, and surrounded by their peers trying to do the same.

That they did produce a lot of music of enduring value is evidenced by the fact that so many of the recordings made in the period Carr wrote about have been reissued on CD and received a warm welcome from new listeners. Perhaps all of the finest music is 'music outside' when new, but eventually audiences catch up. Some of the music of the sixties and early seventies, in retrospect, listened to on record, detached from the atmosphere of time and place, sounds raw and experimental, rough and unfinished; there was an urgency about getting ideas out when so much was in flux and musical developments were so rapid. But most of this music holds up very well indeed. And the best musicians from that time not only produced some timeless recorded music then but, in many cases, went on to even greater achievements later.

One thing that several of them did, and which had not really been the case with the previous British modern jazz generation, was to set their gaze firmly on Europe and go out to make their music known abroad through collaborations with Continental musicians, appearances on the

Continent with their own bands, and frequent recordings on record labels well organised for international distribution. Manfred Eicher's ECM label in Germany has been of great importance for musicians such as John Surman, Kenny Wheeler and John Taylor, carrying their music to a wide international market. But among the previous generation of British musicians — although European opportunities were taken if they arose — the eyes of the most ambitious players were always set on the United States. Tubby Hayes recorded in New York, and much British excitement accompanied the release of albums by Don Rendell and Joe Harriott in America. But, except in the case of those few who emigrated and really succeeded as jazz instrumentalists (like Victor Feldman, Marian McPartland and George Shearing), the United States remained largely uninterested in Brits who played jazz.

Music Outside is very much a story of transition, of a musical world opening up, and Ian Carr's purpose was to alert readers to important cultural developments that, at the time, were being insufficiently noticed. Putting the book into a longer time perspective, with all the advantages of hindsight after thirty years, it is interesting to see what he emphasised and what he skated over or did not notice in the text. Joe Harriott is mentioned briefly as the totally neglected figure he then was. Now, three decades on, he has widening recognition in Britain and abroad as a great pioneer of contemporary jazz and many of his records are available again. But his 'abstract music' at the beginning of the 1960s — a free form jazz that was free enough to include free improvisation, modal improvisation and bop as required — clearly was a false start in historical terms. It took another half decade before the kinds of musical freedom he used so successfully in his quintet began to filter into the jazz of the 'music outside' generation. Why

Harriott had apparently so little influence on a development that occurred so soon after his classic *Free Form* and
Abstract albums were issued is not discussed in this book,
and the question still remains unanswered.

There were other straws in the wind at the very beginning of the sixties. The charismatic Graham Bond is discussed in the chapter on Jon Hiseman. In 1961 Bond
joined the frontline of Don Rendell's quintet which made
the 1961 album *Roarin'* (now reissued on CD). Carr mentions the album but not the bizarre combination on it of
Rendell's elegant bop tenor style and Bond's blues-
drenched alto playing with its split notes, exaggerated
smears and rough, vocalised sounds. Bond was billed as
the 'wild man' of the group. He left it in 1962 to concentrate on playing organ and piano and eventually to form his
own rhythm and blues group. Was this another false start
in moving towards the more open approaches of contemporary jazz? Bond felt confined by modern jazz, but
Rendell was trying to open it up. Don Rendell appears in
Music Outside as co-leader of the Rendell–Carr Quintet,
one of the most important British modern jazz groups of
the late 1960s. Carr writes of his own eventual need to
escape the group's constraints and of how his introduction
into the quintet of the 'wildly exotic' Guy Warren merely
pointed up the incongruities. But the earlier Bond–
Rendell episode points up the lesson that the most imaginative musicians are usually in the business of trying to
escape the constraints of the idiom that provides their language of expression.

What has happened to the musicians who feature so
memorably in the pages of Ian Carr's book? It is impossible here to follow all of them through their later careers but
some main characters can be mentioned, to try to extend a
little way the story the book tells. Perhaps inevitably, in

such a high-risk business as that of making cutting-edge music there were tragedies and casualties, the ones who did not survive. Ian Carr mentions three major modern jazz figures who died, still young, shortly before the book appeared — Tubby Hayes, Phil Seamen and Joe Harriott. The enigmatic but much respected pianist and composer Mike Taylor had also died in 1969 aged thirty-one. Graham Bond was thirty-six at his death in 1975 and South African expatriate trumpeter Mongezi Feza was only thirty when he died in December of the same year. In all these cases, their conditions of life had something, or everything, to do with their demise.

I first heard 'Mongs' with Chris McGregor's Blue Notes in London in 1965, when the band had just arrived from the Continent, but the image of Feza that stays in my mind is from around 1974–75 at the 100 Club in London's Oxford Street, where he often played with various groups. In an interval between sets he was wolfing down a plate of the club's Chinese food, sitting in the shadows at the side of the stage, a seemingly lonely figure ignoring the other musicians. Small and slight, and a fine, explosive player, he

Dudu
Pukwana

worked in Elton Dean's, Harry Miller's and Keith Tippett's bands and with Dudu Pukwana's Spear and the Brotherhood of Breath.

As Ian Carr makes clear, the South African expatriates — exiled from their homeland to escape the consequences of apartheid — had a huge influence on the British contemporary jazz scene in the 1970s. Of the original Blue Notes, bassist Johnny Dyani stayed for the shortest time in Britain, moving to Copenhagen in 1971 and playing with such international stars as Archie Shepp, Abdullah Ibrahim (Dollar Brand) and David Murray. Chris McGregor moved from Britain to France in 1974 to live in an old water mill, growing his own food and farming wheat — aiming for self-sufficiency. He continued to lead the Brotherhood of Breath, re-assembling it regularly for particular engagements and tours almost up to the time of his death in 1990 and still drawing most its personnel from the ranks of British players and the South African expats. Blue Notes altoist Dudu Pukwana remained in the UK, leading his own bands from the late 1970s until his death in 1990. Only drummer Louis Moholo still survives from the original Blue Notes quintet (Dyani died in Berlin in 1986, aged forty). In the decades since Ian Carr wrote, Moholo has led his own groups and worked in numerous associations with many of the strongest contemporary British and Continental improvisers, becoming a widely respected elder statesman of European contemporary jazz and improvised music.

Among other South Africans in London in the period Carr writes about, bassist Harry Miller gets few mentions in *Music Outside* but quickly became a very important figure in the British and European contemporary jazz scene, working with many groups and leading his own Isipingo band (including Feza, Moholo, trombonist Nick Evans,

altoist Mike Osborne and pianist Keith Tippett) in the
1970s. He was not part of the Blue Notes but worked fre-
quently with the Brotherhood of Breath. Miller moved to
the Netherlands in the late 1970s to be close to some of his
then closest musical associates. But he died prematurely in
a car crash in 1983.

The theme of careers cut short could be continued ad
nauseam. The magnificent Mike Osborne, for example,
who appears in retrospect as one of the giants of the 'music
outside' generation, was absent from the music scene,
through illness, after around 1980*. But tragedy should
not be allowed to hide the real triumphs. When Carr
wrote, Osborne may have seemed just one of many interesting soloists. But during the 1970s he emerged as one
of the most adventurous players in a style labelled freebop, combining strong rhythms and intricate, technically
dazzling playing with a completely open approach to
improvisation. With his trio (especially with Miller on bass
and Moholo on drums) he produced fiercely original
music (captured on the 1974 *Border Crossing* and 1975
All Night Long albums) and he was always in demand to
play in contemporary groups on the London scene. In
1974–75, he joined two other leading saxophonists, Alan
Skidmore and John Surman, in a trio, SOS. The mark it
made in its brief existence confirmed the standing these
three players now had as the leading saxophonists in
British contemporary jazz.

Skidmore, and especially Surman, have gone on to
illustrious careers as international stars in Europe and
beyond. Both set their sights, from the end of the 1960s,
on establishing themselves with European audiences and
both have worked extensively on the Continent. While

---

* News of his death in September 2007 arrived as this book was going to press.

they have kept their career profiles high over the years, both have made clear that they could not have done so had they tried to rely on work opportunities in Britain. Skidmore said in 1981, "There's no scene for me in England as a professional jazz musician . . . now I just work in Europe." He played with the West German Radio Orchestra, Elvin Jones, and extensively with German bassist Ali Haurand in co-led or co-operative groups. Of course, Skidmore, like Surman, performs in Britain too, but both of them exemplify the totally international outlook of the leading figures of the 'music outside' generation. Surman has built a massive, well-deserved reputation worldwide, through well-judged projects and appearances (having rejected the kind of frantic international touring that wore him out in the three years with The Trio to 1972). His recording activity for ECM has been prolific, with many albums under his own name and for other leaders. So his public profile has always been strong. Underpinning all this have been long-term projects, such as his work in Paris for the Carolyn Carlson Dance Company throughout the second half of the 1970s, the 'Brass Project' with John Warren, and a longstanding collaboration with Norwegian singer Karin Krog. Choosing his work with care and always making sure of its impact, Surman is as far from the stereotype of the gigging British jazzman as it is possible to get.

Among other players who have consolidated their reputation by similar means is trumpeter Kenny Wheeler. His international reputation matches Surman's and he has also recorded prolifically, being given the freedom, especially by ECM, to present his own projects on record and consolidate his high reputation as a jazz composer for large and small groups. Always in international demand as a trumpeter and flugelhorn player in the decades since Carr wrote, he has played with almost all the leading figures in contemporary jazz and, keeping an open mind about musical styles and idioms, has worked as comfortably with the most radical of free improvisers as with big bands and contemporary jazz groups.

These are examples of outstanding success stories — in musical if not necessarily financial terms — among the instrumentalists discussed in *Music Outside*. Many other players too have made their impact as internationally known musicians. Pianist Gordon Beck and drummer John Marshall are examples, working in Europe and touring well beyond, Beck mainly with his trios and as a soloist, Marshall with German bassist Eberhard Weber in the late 1970s, Ian Carr's Nucleus in the eighties and more recently with Surman, Mike Gibbs and others. That something fresh and important was being shaped during the years Carr wrote about has been amply proved by the development of the music and the attention it has since gathered in Britain but especially beyond the UK.

Carr went out of his way in *Music Outside* to include coverage of the 'sharp end' of contemporary improvised music by devoting chapters to Evan Parker, John Stevens and Trevor Watts. These chapters are specially valuable for the light they shed on the complex relations of free improvisers like Parker and Derek Bailey with the exponents of conservatory-influenced 'contemporary straight music', as Carr calls it, and with what became the more mainstream developments in contemporary jazz. Interestingly, Carr admitted some years after *Music Outside* was published that "Derek and Evan — I like both very much but I'm not interested in their music at all." It is, nonetheless, a great tribute to Carr as an author and musician that his discussion of the 'improv' players, their music and their outlook, is so sensitive and enlightening.

The greater integration of the music scene that he may have been hoping for — and which his book seems to encourage with its focus on key figures like Parker and Stevens who straddled the jazz and improv camps easily — does not seem to have happened in the past three decades. Parker has become a greatly respected figure internationally and remains highly active as a leading free improviser. While he has played in many combinations with British, American and European musicians, much of his work, like Bailey's, has been as a solo improviser.

John Stevens, full of enthusiasm and energy to spread the joys of music making in many different contexts, led such varied organisations as his Dance Orchestra and the jazz-rock group Away in the 1970s and his Freebop group in the eighties, and continued to teach, organise community projects, and inspire other players until his death in 1994. Trevor Watts has also followed an eclectic path with his Amalgam band combining aspects of jazz, improv, folk and rock. From the 1980s, various editions of his Moiré Music groups incorporated African elements with a heavy emphasis on drums. Derek Bailey, throughout the decades up to his death in 2005, pursued his own utterly uncompromising path and organised his Company festival of free improvisers regularly from 1976 until the 1990s. He set down his thoughts about musical improvisation in an important text first published in 1980 and his uniqueness as a musician is captured in Ben Watson's 2004 book about him. Among other musicians who have been important in bridging wide areas of the British contemporary jazz spectrum, especially its 'freer' regions, composer and pianist Keith Tippett also deserves mention, particularly for a succession of large-scale orchestra projects such as Ark and Tapestry and the free improvising of his Ovary Lodge and Mujician groups.

Ian Carr gave special prominence in *Music Outside* to Mike Westbrook and Mike Gibbs as leading jazz composers. Gibbs is rightly portrayed as a musician of great integrity able to function in many musical idioms. This flexibility has enabled him to operate effectively since the mid—1970s as a composer and arranger in many contexts, including work for films and the stage. In 1974 he moved to the United States to become composer-in-residence at his alma mater, the Berklee School of Music, staying in the job until 1983. Over the years he has often presented his music in Britain and on the Continent with specially organised big bands or with radio orchestras. One of his finest achievements is his *Europeana Suite* recorded in 1994 by pianist Joachim Kuhn, the Hannover Radio Philharmonic Orchestra, and a galaxy of top jazz soloists. Gibbs' achingly beautiful, endlessly varied scoring of folk songs from across Europe transcends musical categories and seems a kind of perfect fulfilment of the totally open approach to music that Carr's chapter highlights.

When *Music Outside* was written, Mike Westbrook had already produced a magnificent body of recorded work — indicated in the discography. Since then, he has done much more, resisting classification, still escaping jazz convention while affirming the truths of the jazz tradition. I was lucky enough to be present at the Phonogram Studios in London in March 1975 when his *Citadel/Room 315* was recorded with a large orchestra featuring John Surman. It was clear at the time that it was something very special and it may well be his finest achievement to date, full of detailed, rich writing, honed already in performance before the album was made. Surman's solo work on the record is truly inspired. But Westbrook was already moving in a different direction in 1974, partly for economic reasons but partly because of his interest in developing

Mike Westbrook (*right*) with Roger Cotterrell, 1975, at the Westbrooks' home in East London (photo Kate Westbrook).

music in new, flexible contexts. His Brass Band, which could perform anywhere and gave new opportunities for his writing talents, was one important result. Beyond that, his long-standing interest in music theatre and mixed media presentations, as well as his openness to musical resources beyond jazz, has led to a huge range of projects with large and small groups. As with so many other musicians, mentioned earlier, his audiences are as much (or more) in Continental Europe as in Britain and he still remains scandalously under-appreciated in his own country for his huge contribution to contemporary music.

Something very similar must be said about Michael Garrick. He gets a cameo portrait in the book mainly as a bandleader and for his work in poetry and jazz, but over the years he has been as tenacious as a composer as Westbrook and no less ambitious. Like Westbrook, Garrick sees himself as firmly within the jazz tradition and loves it deeply but equally recognises no fixed musical boundaries. He draws in his most ambitious compositions on whatever seems appropriate from any musical idioms that interest him and serve his purposes. Some of the most striking of these compositions, defying all musical categorisation, such as *Judas Kiss* (1970), *Zodiac of Angels* (1988) and *Bovington Poppies* (1993) still await issue on record. He uses choirs, strings, recited texts and poetry and his large-scale works combine powerful jazz improvisations with composed textures that often evoke very English musical images. The good news is that, like so many of the key players and composers that Carr wrote about, Garrick has had the encouragement of seeing many of his records reissued on CD in recent years. The prophet doesn't have enough honour in his own country but is getting more than before.

Among other composers, Neil Ardley and Graham Collier certainly deserve mention. Ardley may have seemed when Carr wrote to have been among the more important jazz composers and he produced a number of major extended works, but in retrospect Garrick and Westbrook are the key figures in broadening the palette of composition to enrich jazz with other musical forms and escaping the tyranny of categories. Perhaps the results of Graham Collier's work have been more uneven but he has been the most ambitious of them all in trying to rethink the whole idea of composition in its relation to jazz improvisation. Like Garrick and Westbrook, he continues to be highly productive as a composer and, like them, has much of his earlier work available again, reissued on CD for today's listeners to judge. For me, his greatest triumph was the star-studded performance of his extended work *Hoarded Dreams* at the Bracknell Jazz Festival in 1983, finally released on record in 2007. And, again like Garrick and Westbrook, Collier's importance has also been as a

facilitator — setting up situations in which creative improvisers can work and be inspired — precisely what, for him,
jazz composing is all about.

What about Ian Carr himself, in the years since *Music
Outside* first appeared? At the end of the book we leave
him excited by new prospects for his jazz-rock band
Nucleus and full of plans. In fact, despite the group's real
success then and later, the mid–1970s were a difficult time
for him. In an interview in 1981 he explained that:

> . . . in 1975 I hated my own playing and writing and so
> what must I do — I must write, for example a biography of
> Miles Davis because I've been asked to do that. And so for
> about two years I did about one tour with Nucleus, but in
> 1976 and most of 1977, I was studying music, the keyboard
> and harmony, everything about it and I was writing the Miles
> Davis book and also analysing his music. And slowly I got
> very depressed. I thought this is the end because I didn't like
> my playing or my writing and I thought maybe I'm never
> going to like it again.

But Carr's book on Davis is now a classic and he went
on to write a fine biography of Keith Jarrett too. His enthusiasm and confidence as a player came back, marked by
the appropriately-titled Nucleus album *Out of the Long
Dark* and many later recordings. In 1975 he also began a
productive twenty-year association with the United Jazz
and Rock Ensemble, a co-operative group of European
musicians organised from Germany, and he played with
American composer George Russell's Living Time
Orchestra and many other bands. In 2006 his own biography, by Alyn Shipton, was published and he received the
BBC award for 'Services to Jazz'.

What then has really changed in jazz in Britain since
Music Outside was written? In musical terms, a great deal.
The musicians Carr wrote about brought much that was

new. They did a huge amount to create jazz idioms that owed much less than before to American models. The 'music outside' generation helped to build a collective self-confidence that made European jazz eventually no longer reliant on American developments; it came to have not just a distinctive flavour but a clear identity of its own. And they broadened the scope of jazz music, enriching it in innumerable ways. The era of the modern jazz 'suits' now seems far away. If there was a downside, perhaps it was that the newness of contemporary jazz encouraged too dismissive attitudes to what had gone before and it is only in the past few years (again through the availability of CD reissues) that it has been possible to reassess the work of many unjustly neglected British and European modern jazz musicians of the 1950s and before. Even Stan Tracey had fallen out of favour when Carr wrote, despite growing musically all the time and eventually taking his place in later decades as one of the cherished stars of British jazz.

In other respects not much has changed since the early 1970s. Jazz in Britain still receives inadequate recognition as part of the national culture. Ambitious musicians must still look abroad for career chances and can hardly rely on adequate opportunities in the United Kingdom. Creative musicians are still fated to suffer disillusionment; they still play often to small, if loyal, audiences. But something else remains constant, too. New musicians emerge all the time, keen to add their voices to the ever-developing jazz tradition. As the British jazz writer Brian Case put it years ago, "We don't deserve it, but the cats, they keep coming." It's still true. Given the timeless validity of musical improvisation it would be surprising if things were any other way.

DISCOGRAPHY (1973)

I. NEIL ARDLEY

Western Reunion: The New Jazz Orchestra
(Decca LK 4690)   1965
Neil Ardley (director), Bob Leaper, Mike Phillipson, Tony Dudley (trumpets), Ian Carr (trumpet/flugelhorn), Mick Palmer (French horn), John Mumford, Paul Rutherford (trombones), Peter Harvey (bass trombone), Dick Hart (tuba), Les Carter (flutes), Trevor Watts (alto sax/flute), Barbara Thompson (alto), Dave Gelly, Tom Harris (tenor saxes), Sebastian Freudenberg (baritone), Mike Barrett (piano), Tony Reeves (bass), Jon Hiseman (drums).

Déjeuner Sur L'Herbe: NJO
(Verve VLP 9236)   1968
Neil Ardley (director), Derek Watkins, Henry Lowther, Harry Beckett, Ian Carr (trumpets/flugelhorns), John Mumford, Mike Gibbs, Derek Wadsworth, Tony Russell (trombones), George Smith (tuba), Barbara Thompson (flute/soprano/alto), Dave Gelly (tenor/clarinet/bass clarinet), Jim Philip (tenor/flute/clarinet), Dick Heckstall-Smith (tenor/soprano), Frank Ricotti (vibes/marimba), Jack Bruce (bass), Jon Hiseman (drums).

Greek Variations: with Ian Carr and Don Rendell
(Columbia SCX 6414)   1969
Neil Ardley (director), Ian Carr (trumpet/flugelhorn), Don Rendell (tenor/soprano/flute), Barbara Thompson (flute/alto/soprano), Karl Jenkins (oboe/baritone/soprano), Brian Smith (tenor/soprano), Stan Robinson (tenor/flute), Mike Gibbs (trombone), Frank Ricotti (vibes/marimba/percussion), Jeff Clyne (bass), Jack Bruce (bass/bass guitar), Neville Whitehead (bass), John Marshall, Trevor Tomkins (drums), Chris Spedding (guitar), Jack Rothstein, Kelly Isaacs, Ken Essex, Charles Tunnell, A. Flemming (strings).

A Symphony of Amaranths (Regal Zonophone SLRZ 1028)   1971
Neil Ardley (director/prepared piano), Derek Watkins, Nigel Carter, Henry Lowther, Harry Beckett (trumpets/flugelhorns), Derek Wadsworth, Ray Premru (trombones), Dick Hart (tuba), Barbara Thompson, Don Rendell,

Dick Heckstall-Smith, Dave Gelly, John Clementson, Benny Gould (reeds), Jack Rothstein, Kelly Isaacs, Erich Gruenberg, Ken Essex, Charles Tunnell, Francis Gabarro (strings), David Snell, Sidonie Goossens (harps), Frank Ricotti (vibes), Stan Tracey (piano/celeste), Dave Gelly (glockenspiel), Karl Jenkins (electric piano), Alan Branscombe (harpsichord), Chris Laurence, Jeff Clyne (basses), Jon Hiseman (drums), Norma Winstone (vocals), Ivor Cutler (speaker).

2. GORDON BECK
Gordon Beck Plus Two Plays Dr Doolittle (Major Minor SML 88)   1968
Gordon Beck (piano), Kenny Baldock (bass), Jackie Dougan (drums).

Gordon Beck Plus Two Plays Half A Jazz Sixpence
(Major Minor SMLP22)   1968
Gordon Beck (piano), Kenny Baldock (bass), Jackie Dougan (drums).

Gyroscope (Morgan SMJI)   1968
Gordon Beck (piano), Jeff Clyne (bass), Tony Oxley (drums).

Experiments With Pops (Major Minor SMLP 21)   1969
Gordon Beck (piano), Jeff Clyne (bass), John McLaughlin (guitar), Tony Oxley (drums).

Beck-Matthewson-Humair Trio (Dire FO 341)   1972
Gordon Beck (piano), Ron Matthewson (bass), Daniel Humair (drums).

3. HARRY BECKETT
Flare Up (Philips 6308026)   1970
Harry Beckett (trumpet/flugelhorn), John Surman (baritone/soprano), Mike Osborne (alto), Alan Skidmore (tenor/soprano), Frank Ricotti (vibes), John Taylor (piano/electric piano), Chris Laurence (bass), John Webb (drums).

Warm Smiles (RCA Victor SF 8225)   1971
Harry Beckett (trumpet/flugelhorn), Mike Osborne (alto), Frank Ricotti (vibes/congas), John Taylor (piano/electric piano), Chris Laurence (bass), John Webb (drums).

Themes For Fega (RCA SF 8264)   1972
Harry Beckett (trumpet/flugelhorn), Alan Skidmore (soprano/tenor), Mike Osborne (alto), Frank Ricotti (vibes/percussion), John Taylor (electric piano), Chris Laurence (bass), John Webb (drums).

4. JACK BRUCE
Things We Like (Polydor Standard 2343033)   1968

Jack Bruce (bass/vocals), John McLaughlin (guitar), Jon Hiseman (drums), Dick Heckstall-Smith (reeds).

Songs For A Tailor (Polydor 583058)   1969
Jack Bruce (bass guitar/keyboards/cello/vocals), Jon Hiseman, John Marshall (drums), Harry Beckett, Henry Lowther (trumpets/flugelhorns), Dick Heckstall-Smith, Art Themen (reeds), Chris Spedding (guitar).

Harmony Row (Polydor 2310107)   1971
Jack Bruce (bass guitar/vocals), Chris Spedding (guitar), John Marshall (drums).

5. IAN CARR/Nucleus
Elastic Rock (Vertigo 6360 008)   1970
Ian Carr (trumpet/flugelhorn), Karl Jenkins (baritone/oboe/piano/electric piano), Brian Smith (tenor/soprano), Chris Spedding (guitar), Jeff Clyne (bass/bass guitar), John Marshall (drums).

We'll Talk About It Later (Vertigo 6360 027)   1970
Ian Carr (trumpet/flugelhorn), Karl Jenkins (baritone/oboe/piano/electric piano), Brian Smith (tenor/soprano), Chris Spedding (guitar/bouzouki), Jeff Clyne (bass/bass guitar), John Marshall (drums).

Solar Plexus (Vertigo 6360 039)   1970
Ian Carr, Kenny Wheeler, Harry Beckett (trumpets/flugelhorns), Brian Smith (tenor/soprano/flute), Tony Roberts (tenor sax/bass clarinet), Karl Jenkins (electric piano/baritone/oboe), Chris Spedding (guitar), Jeff Clyne (bass/bass guitar), Ron Matthewson (bass guitar), John Marshall (drums/percussion), Chris Karan (percussion), Keith Winter (VCS3 electronic synthesizer).

Belladonna (Vertigo 6360 076)   1972
Ian Carr (trumpet/flugelhorn), Brian Smith (tenor/soprano/alto flute/bamboo flute), Dave MacRae (electric piano), Alan Holdsworth (guitar), Roy Babbington (bass guitar), Gordon Beck (electric piano), Clive Thacker (drums), Trevor Tomkins (percussion).

Labyrinth (Vertigo 6360 091)   1973
Ian Carr, Kenny Wheeler (trumpets/flugelhorns), Norma Winstone (vocals), Tony Coe (bass clarinet/tenor), Brian Smith (tenor/soprano/flute), Dave MacRae, Gordon Beck (electric pianos), Roy Babbington (bass guitar), Clive Thacker, Tony Levin (drums), Trevor Tomkins (percussion), Paddy Kingsland (VCS3 electronic synthesizer).

Roots (Vertigo 6360 100)   1973
Ian Carr (trumpet), Brian Smith (tenor/soprano/flute/bamboo flute), Dave
MacRae (piano, electric piano), Jocelyn Pitchen (guitar), Roger Sutton (bass-
guitar), Clive Thacker (drums), Aureo De Souza (percussion), Joy Yates
(vocals).

6. TONY COE
Tony Coe (Dobells 77 Records)   1971
Tony Coe (reeds), Brian Lemon (piano), Dave Green (bass), Phil Seamen
(drums).

7. GRAHAM COLLIER
Deep Dark Blue Centre (Deram DML 1005)   1967
Graham Collier (bass), Harry Beckett, Kenny Wheeler (trumpets/flugel-
horns), Mike Gibbs (trombone), Dave Aaron (alto/flute), Karl Jenkins (bari-
tone/oboe), Phil Lee (guitar), John Marshall (drums).

Down Another Road (Fontana SFJL 922)   1969
Graham Collier (bass), Harry Beckett (trumpet/flugelhorn), Nick Evans
(trombone), Stan Sulzman (reeds), Karl Jenkins (piano/oboe), John Marshall
(drums).

Songs For My Father (Fontana 6309 006)   1970
Graham Collier (bass), Harry Beckett (trumpet/flugelhorn), Alan Skidmore,
Alan Wakeman, Bob Sydor, Tony Roberts (reeds), Phil Lee (guitar), Derek
Wadsworth (trombone), John Taylor (piano), John Webb (drums).

Mosaics (Fontana 6308 051)   1971
Graham Collier (bass), Harry Beckett (trumpet/flugelhorn), Alan Wakeman,
Bob Sydor (reeds), Geoff Castle (piano), John Webb (drums).

Portraits (Saydisc SDL 244)   1972
Graham Collier (bass), Dick Pearce (flugelhorn), Peter Hurt (alto), Ed Speight
(guitar), Geoff Castle (piano), John Webb (drums).

8. ELTON DEAN
Elton Dean (CBS 64539)   1971
Elton Dean (alto sax/saxello/electric piano), Marc Charig (cornet), Neville
Whitehead (bass guitar), Mike Ratledge (keyboards), Roy Babbington (bass),
Phil Howard (drums).

9. BOB DOWNES
Dream Journey (Philips SBL 7922)   1969
Bob Downes (flute/tenor/Chinese bells), Derek Hogg (percussion), Denis

Smith (drums/percussion), John Stevens (drums), Harry Miller (bass), Jim Gregory (flute), John Warren (baritone), Clive Stevens (tenor), Chris Pyne (trombone), Nigel Carter, Henry Lowther, Butch Hudson (trumpets), Chris Spedding (guitar).

Electric City (Vertigo 6360 005)   1970
Bob Downes (vocals/saxophones/flutes), Dave Brooks (tenor sax), Don Faye (baritone), Nigel Carter, Kenny Wheeler (trumpets), Bud Parks, Harry Beckett, Ian Carr (trumpets/flugelhorns), Ray Russell, Chris Spedding (guitars), Herbie Flowers, Daryl Runswick, Harry Miller (bass guitars), Denis Smith, Alan Rushton, Clem Catini (drums), Robin Jones (congas/timbales).

Deep Down Heavy (Music For Pleasure EMI MFP)   1970
Bob Downes (vocals/sax/flutes), Robert Cockburn (speaker), Chris Spedding, Ray Russell, Peter Billam (guitars), Harry Miller (bass), Laurie Allen, Alan Rushton, Derek Hogg (drums).

Diversions (Openian BDOM 001)   1973
Bob Downes (flutes/tenor/inside piano/percussion/vocal), Barry Guy (bass), Jeff Clyne (bass), Denis Smith (drums), Laurie Baker (synthesizer).

10. AMANCIO D'SILVA
Integration (Columbia SX 6322)   1969
Amancio D'Silva (guitar), Ian Carr (trumpet/flugelhorn), Don Rendell (tenor/soprano), Dave Green (bass), Trevor Tomkins (drums).

Reflections (Columbia SCX 6465)   1970
Amancio D'Silva (guitar) with orchestral accompaniment directed by David Mack, Stan Tracey and Leon Young.

Dream Sequence: Cosmic Eye (Columbia SLR 21030)   1972
Amancio D'Silva (guitar), V. Jasani (sitar), John Mayer (violin), Ray Swinfield (flute), Dave Grossmith (alto flute), C. Taylor (bass flute), Alan Branscombe (saxophone/percussion), T. Campo (bass guitar), Keshav Sathe (tabla), D. Wright (drums). (See also Joe Harriott — *Hum Dono*).

11. MICHAEL GARRICK
A Case Of Jazz (Airborne)   1963
Michael Garrick (piano), Shake Keane (trumpet), Coleridge Goode (bass).

Poetry And Jazz In Concert (Argo ZDA 26/27)   1963
Michael Garrick (piano), Joe Harriott (alto), Shake Keane (trumpet), John Taylor (bass), Colin Barnes (drums).

Moonscape (Airborne)   1964
Michael Garrick (piano), Dave Green, John Taylor (basses), Colin Barnes
(drums).

October Woman (Argo ZDA 33)   1964
Michael Garrick (piano), Joe Harriott (alto), Shake Keane (trumpet), Coleridge
Goode (bass), Colin Barnes (drums).

Promises (Argo ZDA 36)   1965
Michael Garrick (piano), Joe Harriott (alto), Ian Carr (trumpet/flugelhorn),
Tony Coe (tenor/clarinet), Coleridge Goode (bass), Dave Green (bass), Colin
Barnes (drums).

Anthem (Argo ZFA 92)   1965
Michael Garrick (piano), Joe Harriott (alto), Shake Keane (trumpet), Coleridge
Goode (bass), Colin Barnes (drums), Simon Preston (organ), The Elizabethan
Singers.

Before Night/Day (Argo EAF 115)   1966
Jeremy Robson (poet), Michael Garrick (piano), Coleridge Goode (bass),
Colin Barnes (drums), Joe Harriott (alto), Ian Carr (trumpet).

Black Marigolds (Argo ZDA 88)   1966
Michael Garrick (piano), Don Rendell (soprano/tenor), Ian Carr
(trumpet/flugelhorn), Joe Harriott (alto), Tony Coe (tenor/clarinet), Dave
Green (bass), Trevor Tomkins, Colin Barnes (drums), John Smith (poet).

Jazz Praises At St Paul's (Airborne NBP 0021)   1968
Michael Garrick (organ), Art Themen (tenor/soprano/clarinet/flute), Jim Philip
(tenor/clarinet/flute), Ian Carr (trumpet/flugelhorn), Coleridge Goode (bass),
John Marshall (drums), The Choir of St Michael the Archangel, Aldershot,
with boys from Farnborough Grammar School and singers from the University
Choir of St Nicholas Leicester, director Ian Imlay, conductor Peter Mound.

Poetry And Jazz In Concert 250 (Argo ZPR 264/5)   1969
Michael Garrick (piano), Don Rendell (reeds), Ian Carr (horns), Art Themen
(reeds), Dave Green (bass), Trevor Tomkins (drums), Dannie Abse, Thomas
Blackburn, Douglas Hill, Spike Milligan, Jeremy Robson, Vernon Scannell,
John Smith (poets).

The Heart Is A Lotus (Argo ZDA 135)   1970
Michael Garrick (piano), Art Themen, Jim Philip, Don Rendell (reeds), Ian
Carr (trumpet/flugelhorn), Dave Green, Coleridge Goode (basses), Trevor
Tomkins (drums), Norma Winstone (vocals).

Mr Smith's Apocalypse (Argo ZAGF 1)   1971
Jazz Cantata, text by John Smith, Michael Garrick (piano), Don Rendell, Art
Themen (reeds), Henry Lowther (trumpet/flugelhorn), Coleridge Goode
(bass), Trevor Tomkins (drums), Norma Winstone (vocals), Betty Mulcahy,
George Murcell (speakers), The Peter Mound Choir, Somerford Junior
School Choir.

Epiphany/Blessed Are The Peacemakers (single) (Argo AFW 105)   1971
Michael Garrick (piano), Don Rendell, Art Themen (reeds), Henry Lowther
(trumpet/flugelhorn), Dave Green, Coleridge Goode (basses), Trevor
Tomkins (drums), Norma Winstone (vocals).

Cold Mountain (Argo ZDA 153)   1972
Michael Garrick (piano), Dave Green (bass), Trevor Tomkins (drums).

Home Stretch Blues (Argo ZDA 154)   1972
Michael Garrick (piano), Art Themen (reeds), Henry Lowther (trumpet/
flugelhorn), Don Rendell (reeds), Dave Green (bass), Trevor Tomkins
(drums), Norma Winstone (vocals).

12. MIKE GIBBS

Michael Gibbs (Deram DML/SML 1063)   1969
Mike Gibbs (musical director), John Wilbraham (piccolo/trumpet), Derek
Watkins, Kenny Wheeler, Henry Lowther, Nigel Carter, Ian Hamer (trum-
pets), Morris Miller (trumpet/French horn), Nicholas Busch, Jim Buck Jnr. ,
Alan Civil, Valerie Smith (French horns), Cliff Hardie, Chris Pyne, Bobby
Lambe, David Horler (trombones), Ray Premru, Ken Goldy, Maurice Gee
(bass trombones), John Surman, Alan Skidmore, Ray Warleigh, Tony
Roberts, Mike Osborne, Duncan Lamont, Barbara Thompson (reeds), Dick
Hart, Martin Fry (tubas), Chris Spedding, Ray Russell (guitars), Jack Bruce,
Brian Odges (bass guitars), John Marshall, Tony Oxley (drums), Frank Ricotti
(percussion), Fred Alexander, Alan Ford (cellos), Mike Pyne, Bob Cornford
(pianos).

Tanglewood 63 (Deram DML/SML 1087)   1970
Mike Gibbs (musical director), Kenny Wheeler, Henry Lowther, Ian Hamer,
Nigel Carter (trumpets/flugelhorns), Chris Pyne, David Horler, Malcolm
Griffiths (trombones), Dick Hart, Alfie Reece (tubas), Tony Roberts, John
Surman, Alan Skidmore, Stan Sulzman, Brian Smith (reeds), John Marshall,
Clive Thacker (drums/percussion), Frank Ricotti (vibes/percussion), Chris
Spedding (guitar), Roy Babbington (bass/bass guitar), Jeff Clyne (bass), Mike
Pyne, John Taylor, Gordon Beck (keyboards), Tony Gilbert, Michael Rennie,
Hugh Bean, George French, Bill Armon, Raymond Moseley, Geoff
Wakefield (violins), Fred Alexander, Allen Ford (cellos).

Just Ahead (Polydor 2683 011) 1972
Mike Gibbs (musical director), Kenny Wheeler, Henry Lowther, Harry Beckett (trumpets/flugelhorns), Chris Pyne (trombone), Malcolm Griffithss (tenor/bass trombones), Geoff Perkins (bass trombone), Ray Warleigh, Stan Sulzman, Alan Skidmore (reeds), Dave MacRae, John Taylor (electric pianos), Chris Spedding (guitar/sitar), Roy Babbington (bass guitar), John Marshall (drums), Frank Ricotti (vibes/percussion).

In The Public Interest (Polydor) 1973
Recorded in New York
Mike Gibbs (musical director), Gary Burton (vibes), Steve Swallow (bass guitar), Mike Brecker (tenor/soprano), Randy Brecker, Marvin Stamm, Jeff Stout, Pat Stout (trumpets), Bill Watrous, Wayne Andre, Paul Felise (trombones), David Taylor (tuba), Pat Rebillot, Al Zovad (keyboards), Mick Goodrick (guitar), George Ricci, Alan Shulman (cellos), Harvey Wainapel, Paul Moen (saxophones), Harry Blazer, Bob Moses (drums).

13. JOE HARRIOTT

Free Form (Jazzland JLP 49) 1960
Joe Harriott (alto), Shake Keane (trumpet/flugelhorn), Pat Smythe (piano), Coleridge Goode (bass), Phil Seamen (drums).

Abstract (Columbia 33SX 1477) 1961/2
Joe Harriott (alto), Shake Keane (trumpet/flugelhorn), Pat Smythe (piano), Coleridge Goode (bass), Phil Seamen, Bobby Orr (drums), Frank Holder (bongos).

Movement (Columbia 33SX 1627) 1963
Joe Harriott (alto), Shake Keane (trumpet/flugelhorn), Pat Smythe (piano), Coleridge Goode (bass), Bobby Orr (drums).

High Spirits (Columbia 33SX 1692) 1964
Joe Harriott (alto), Shake Keane (trumpet/flugelhorn), Pat Smythe (piano), Coleridge Goode (bass), Bobby Orr (drums).

Indo-Jazz Suite 1965
Joe Harriott (alto), Eddie Blair (trumpet), Chris Taylor (flute), Pat Smythe (piano), Rick Laird (bass), Alan Ganley (drums), John Mayer (violin), Diwan Motihar (sitar), Keshav Sathe (tabla), Chandrahas Paiganhar (tamboora).

Indo-Jazz Fusions (Columbia SX 6122)   1966
Joe Harriott (alto), Shake Keane (trumpet), Chris Taylor (flute), Pat Smythe (piano), Coleridge Goode (bass), Alan Ganley (drums), John Mayer (violin), Diwan Motihar (sitar), Keshav Sathe (tabla), Chandrahas Paiganhar (tamboora).

Swings High (Melodisc SLP 12-150)   1967
Joe Harriott (alto), Stu Hamer (trumpet/flugelhorn), Pat Smythe (piano), Coleridge Goode (bass), Phil Seamen (drums).

Indo-Jazz Fusions II (Columbia SX 6215)   1967
Joe Harriott (alto), Kenny Wheeler (trumpet/flugelhorn), Chris Taylor (flute), Pat Smythe (piano), Coleridge Goode (bass), Jackie Dougan (drums), John Mayer (violin), Diwan Motihar (sitar), Keshav Sathe (tabla), Chandrahas Paiganhar (tamboora).

Hum Dono: with Amancio D'Silva (Columbia 6354)   1969
Joe Harriott (alto), Amancio D'Silva (guitar), Norma Winstone (vocals), Ian Carr (trumpet/flugelhorn), Dave Green (bass), Bryan Spring (drums).

14. TUBBY HAYES
Tubby Hayes and his Orchestra (Tempo EXA 14)   1955
Jimmy Deuchar, Dickie Hawdon (trumpets), Mike Senn (alto/baritone), Tubby Hayes (tenor), Jackie Sharpe (tenor/baritone), Harry South (piano), Pete Blannin (bass), Lennie Breslaw (drums).

Tubby Hayes Quartet (Tempo EXA 2728)   1955
Tubby Hayes (tenor), Harry South (piano), Pete Blannin (bass), Bill Eyden (drums).

Tubby Hayes and his Orchestra (Tempo TAP 2)   February 1956
Tubby Hayes and his Orchestra (Tempo EXA 36)   February 1956
Ian Hamer, Dickie Hawdon (trumpets), Mike Senn (alto), Tubby Hayes (tenor), Jackie Sharpe (baritone), Harry South (piano), Pete Blannin (bass), Bill Eyden (drums), Bobby Breen (congas).

Tubby Hayes Quintet (Tempo TAP 6)   1956
Dickie Hawdon (trumpet), Tubby Hayes (tenor), Harry South (piano), Pete Elderfield (bass), Bill Eyden (drums).

Tubby Hayes and the Jazz Couriers (Tempo TAP 15)   1957
Tubby Hayes (tenor/vibes), Ronnie Scott (tenor), Terry Shannon (piano), Phil Bates (bass), Bill Eyden (drums).

In Concert (Tempo TAP 22)   1958
Tubby Hayes (tenor/vibes), Ronnie Scott (tenor), Terry Shannon (piano), Phil
Bates (bass), Bill Eyden (drums).

The Eighth Wonder (Tempo EXA 82)   1958
Tubby Hayes (altos/tenor/baritone/vibes/piano) multi-recording.

Tubby Hayes and the Jazz Couriers (London LTZ L15188)   1958
Tubby Hayes (tenor), Ronnie Scott (tenor), Terry Shannon (piano), Jeff Clyne
(bass), Bill Eyden (drums).

The Last Word (Tempo TAP 26)   1959
Tubby Hayes (flute/tenor/vibes), Ronnie Scott (tenor), Terry Shannon
(piano), Kenny Napper (bass), Phil Seamen (drums).

Tubby's Groove (Tempo TAP 29)   December 1959
Tubby Hayes (tenor/vibes), Terry Shannon (piano), Jeff Clyne (bass), Phil
Seamen (drums).

Tubbs (Fontana TFL 5142)   1960/1961
Tubby Hayes (tenor), Terry Shannon (piano), Jeff Clyne (bass), Bill Eyden
(drums), Bobby Pratt, Stan Roderick, Eddie Blair, Jimmy Deuchar (trumpets),
Don Lusher, Jimmy Wilson, Keith Christie, Ray Premru (trombones), Alfie
Reece (tuba), Johnny Scott (piccolo), Jimmy Scott (flute/alto flute), Bill Skeat
(flute/clarinet), Bob Burns, Al Newman (clarinets/bass clarinets), Harry
Meyers (oboe), Dave Goldberg (guitar).

Tubby Hayes Quartet (Fontana TFL 5151)   1961
Tubby Hayes (tenor/vibes), Terry Shannon (piano), Jeff Clyne (bass), Bill
Eyden (drums).

Tubbs in NY (Fontana TFL 5183)   1961
Clark Terry (trumpet), Tubby Hayes (tenor), Horace Parlan (piano), Eddie
Costa (vibes), George Duvivier (bass), Dave Bailey (drums).

Late Spot At Scott's (Fontana TL 5200)   1962
Jimmy Deuchar (trumpet), Tubby Hayes (tenor/soprano/vibes), Gordon Beck
(piano), Freddy Logan (bass), Alan Ganley (drums).

Down In The Village (Fontana 680998 TL)   1962
Jimmy Deuchar (trumpet), Tubby Hayes (tenor/soprano/vibes), Gordon Beck
(piano), Freddy Logan (bass), Alan Ganley (drums).

Tubby Hayes And The Allstars: Return Visit (Fontana TL 5195)   1962
Tubby Hayes (tenor/vibes), James Moody (Jimmy Gloomy) (tenor/flute),
Roland Kirk (tenor/noseflute/manzello/stritch), Walter Bishop (piano), Sam
Jones (bass), Louis Hayes (drums).

Tubbs' Tours (Fontana TL 5221)   1964
Jimmy Deuchar (trumpet/mellophonium), Ian Hamer, Les Condon (trum-
pets), Keith Christie (trombone), Ken Wray (valve trombone), Ronnie Ross
(alto/baritone/bass clarinet), Tubby Hayes (flute/tenor/vibes), Peter King,
Bobby Wellins (tenor/clarinet), Jackie Sharpe (baritone/clarinet), Terry
Shannon (piano), Freddy Logan (bass), Alan Ganley (drums).

100% Proof (Fontana TL 5410)   1966
Kenny Baker, Ian Hamer, Greg Bowen, Les Condon, Kenny Wheeler (trum-
pets), Keith Christie, Nat Peck, Johnny Marshall, Chris Smith (trombones),
Roy Willox, Ray Warleigh (altos/flutes), Ronnie Scott (tenor/clarinet), Tubby
Hayes (tenor/flute/vibes), Bob Efford (tenor/oboe/flute/bass clarinet), Ronnie
Ross (baritone/bass clarinet), Gordon Beck (piano), Jeff Clyne (bass), Ronnie
Stevenson (drums), Harry Klein (baritone), Johnny Butts (drums).

Jazz Tête-A-Tête (77 LEU 12/21)   1966
Les Condon (trumpet), Tubby Hayes (tenor), Mike Pyne (piano), Ron
Matthewson (bass).

Mexican Green (Fontana SFJL 911)   1967
Tubby Hayes (flute/tenor), Mike Pyne (piano), Ron Matthewson (bass), Tony
Levin (drums).

The Tubby Hayes Orchestra (Fontana 6309 002)   1969
Derek Watkins, Greg Bowen, Tony Fisher, Ian Hamer (trumpets), Keith
Christie, David Horler, Bill Geldard (trombones), Roy Willox (alto), Tubby
Hayes (flute/tenor), Bob Efford (tenor/woodwind), Alan Branscombe
(piano/vibes/percussion), Louis Stewart (guitar), Ron Matthewson (bass
guitar), Spike Wells (drums), plus harp, eight violins, two violas, two cellos.

15. JON HISEMAN/Colosseum
Those Who Are About To Die (Philips STL 5510)   1968/69
Dick Heckstall-Smith (reeds), James Litherland (vocals/guitar), Tony Reeves
(bass guitar), Dave Greenslade (organ), Jon Hiseman (drums).

Valentyne Suite (Vertigo VO1)   1969
Dick Heckstall-Smith (reeds), James Litherland (vocals/guitar), Tony Reeves
(bass guitar), Dave Greenslade (organ), Jon Hiseman (drums).

The Grass Is Greener (Dunhill DS 50079)   1969
Dick Heckstall-Smith (reeds), James Litherland (vocals/guitar), Tony Reeves
(bass guitar), Dave Clempson (vocals/guitar), Dave Greenslade (organ), Jon
Hiseman (drums).

The Daughter Of Time (Vertigo 6360017)   1970
Dick Heckstall-Smith, Barbara Thompson (reeds), Mark Clark (bass guitar),
Derek Wadsworth (trombone), Harry Beckett (trumpet/flugelhorn), Dave
Clempson (guitar/vocals), Jon Hiseman (drums), Jack Rothstein, Trevor
Williams, Nicholas Kramer, Charles Tunnell, Fred Alexander (strings), Chris
Farlowe (vocals), Dave Greenslade (organ), featuring some arrangements by
Neil Ardley.

Colosseum Live (Bronze ICD 1/2)   1971
Dick Heckstall-Smith (reeds), Dave Greenslade (organ), Dave Clempson (gui-
tar/vocals), Mark Clark (bass guitar/vocals), Chris Farlowe (vocals), Jon
Hiseman (drums).

Collectors Colosseum (Bronze ILPS 9173)   1968–71
A compilation of previously unreleased tracks made during the above sessions.
The personnel are variously as above.

16. INCUS
The Topography of The Lungs (Incus 1)   1970
Evan Parker (saxophones), Derek Bailey (guitar), Han Bennink (percussion).

Solo Guitar
(Incus 2)   1971
Derek Bailey (guitar/VCS3 electronic synthesizer).

Iskra 1903 (Incus 3/4)   1970/72
Paul Rutherford (trombone/piano), Derek Bailey (acoustic/amplified guitar),
Barry Guy (acoustic/amplified bass).

Collective Calls (Urban) (Two Microphones) (Incus 5)   1972
Evan Parker (soprano/homemade instruments/cassette recorder), Paul
Lytton (percussion/live electronics/sound effects/noise).

Ode (Incus 6/7)   1972
The London Jazz Composers Orchestra: Harry Beckett, Dave Holdsworth,
Marc Charig (trumpets/flugelhorns), Paul Nieman, Paul Rutherford, Mike
Gibbs (trombones), Dick Hart (tuba), Mike Osborne, Bernie Living (altos),
Evan Parker, Alan Wakeman (tenors/sopranos), Trevor Watts (alto/soprano),
Bob Downes (flute), Karl Jenkins (oboe/baritone), Howard Riley (piano),

Derek Bailey (guitar), Barry Guy, Chris Laurence, Jeff Clyne (basses), Paul Lytton, Tony Oxley (drums/live electronics), Buxton Orr (conductor).

The Music Improvisation Company
(ECM 1005 – distributed in Britain by Incus)   1970
Derek Bailey (electric guitar), Evan Parker (soprano saxophone), Hugh Davies (live electronics), Jamie Muir (percussion), Christine Jeffrey (voice).

17. PETE LEMER
Local Colour (ESP Disc 1057)   1966
Pete Lemer (piano), Nisar Ahmed, (George) Khan, John Surman (reeds), Jon Hiseman (drums), Tony Reeves (bass).

18. HENRY LOWTHER
Child Song (Deram SML 1070)   1970
Henry Lowther (trumpet/flugelhorn/violin/percussion), Tony Roberts (tenor/bass clarinet/percussion), Mike McNaught (electric piano/percussion), Daryl Runswick (bass/bass guitar/percussion), Mike Travis (drums/percussion), Jimmy Jewell (tenor), Neil Slaven (percussion).

19. CHRIS McGREGOR
Cold Castle Jazz Festival (Gallojazz)   1963
Chris McGregor's band on two tracks.

The African Sound (Gallojazz)   1963
Chris McGregor (piano), Kippie Moeketsi (alto/clarinet), Dudu Pukwana (alto), Ronnie Beer (tenor), Nikele Moyake (tenor), Barney Rabachane (alto), Chris Ngeutane (baritone), Mongezi Feza, Dennis Mpali, Ebbie Creswell, Noel Jones (trumpets), Bob Tizzard, Blyth Mbityana, Willy Nettle (trombones), Sammy Moritz (bass), Early Mabuac (drums).

Kwela (Dobells 77 Records)   1967/8
Chris McGregor (piano), Dudu Pukwana (alto), Ronnie Beer (tenor), Coleridge Goode (bass), Laurie Allen (drums).

Up to Earth (Polydor 583072–unreleased)   1968
Chris McGregor (piano), Dudu Pukwana (alto), Mongezi Feza (trumpet), Evan Parker (tenor), John Surman (baritone), Barre Phillips, Danny Thompson (basses), Louis Moholo (drums).

Very Urgent (Polydor 184137)   1968
Chris McGregor (piano), Ronnie Beer (tenor), Dudu Pukwana (alto), Mongezi Feza (trumpet), Johnny Dyani (bass), Louis Moholo (drums).

Brotherhood Of Breath (RCA Neon NE 2)   1970
Chris McGregor (piano), Malcolm Malcolm Griffithsss, Nick Evans (trombones), Mongezi Feza, Marc Charig, Harry Beckett (trumpets/flugelhorns), Dudu Pukwana, Ronnie Beer, Alan Skidmore, Mike Osborne, John Surman (saxophones), Harry Miller (bass), Louis Moholo (drums).

Brotherhood Of Breath – Brotherhood (RCA Victor SF 8260)   1971
Chris McGregor (piano), Malcolm Griffiths, Nick Evans (trombones), Mongezi Feza, Marc Charig, Harry Beckett (trumpets/flugelhorns), Dudu Pukwana, Alan Skidmore, Mike Osborne, Gary Windo (saxophones), Harry Miller (bass), Louis Moholo (drums).

20. JOHN McLAUGHLIN
Extrapolation (Marmalade 608007)   1969
John McLaughlin (guitar), John Surman (baritone/soprano), Brian Odges (bass), Tony Oxley (drums).

The Inner Mounting Flame: Mahavishnu Orchestra (CBS KC 31067) 1971
John McLaughlin (guitar), Jerry Goodman (violin), Jan Hammer (piano), Rick Laird (bass), Billy Cobham (drums).

Birds Of Fire: Mahavishnu Orchestra (CBS 65321)   1972
John McLaughlin (guitar), Billy Cobham (drums), Rick Laird (bass), Jan Hammer (piano), Jerry Goodman (violin).

21. MIKE OSBORNE
Outback (Turtle TUR 300)   1970
Mike Osborne (alto), Harry Beckett (trumpet/flugelhorn), Chris McGregor (piano), Harry Miller (bass), Louis Moholo (drums).

22. TONY OXLEY
The Baptised Traveller (CBS 52664)   1969
Evan Parker (tenor), Kenny Wheeler (trumpet/flugelhorn), Derek Bailey (guitar), Jeff Clyne (bass), Tony Oxley (drums).

Four Compositions For Sextet (CBS 64071)   1970
Tony Oxley (drums), Derek Bailey (guitar), Evan Parker (tenor), Kenny Wheeler (trumpet/flugelhorn), Paul Rutherford (trombone), Jeff Clyne (bass).

Icnos (RCA 8215)   1972
Tony Oxley (drums/percussion), Evan Parker (tenor), Kenny Wheeler (trumpet/flugelhorn), Derek Bailey (guitar), Paul Rutherford (trombone), Barry Guy (bass).

23. DON RENDELL

Don Rendell Sextet (Tempo EP EXA 16) 1954
Dickie Hawdon (trumpet/flugelhorn), Don Rendell, Ronnie Ross (tenors), Damian Robinson (piano), Ashley Kozack (bass), Derek Hogg (drums).

Jazz At The Festival Hall (Decca EP LK 4087) 1954
Dickie Hawdon (trumpet/flugelhorn), Don Rendell (tenor), Ronnie Ross (baritone), Damian Robinson (piano), Pete Elderfield (bass), Benny Goodman (drums).

Don Rendell Sextet (Tempo EP EXA 12) 1955
Dickie Hawdon (trumpet/flugelhorn), Don Rendell (tenor), Ronnie Ross (baritone), Damian Robinson (piano), Pete Elderfield (bass), Don Lawson (drums).

Don Rendell Quartet (Tempo EP EXA 11) 1955
Don Rendell (tenor), Damian Robinson (piano), Pete Elderfield (bass), Don Lawson (drums).

Don Rendell–Bobby Jaspar (Vogue LP LDE 144) 1955
Don Rendell, Bobby Jaspar (tenors), Dave Amram (French horn), Maurice Vander (piano), Sacha Distel (guitar), Guy Pedersen (bass), Jean-Baptiste 'Mac Kac' Reilles (drums), Christian Chevallier (composer/ arranger).

Meet Don Rendell (Tempo LAP 1) 1955
Don Rendell (tenor), Damian Robinson (piano), Sammy Stokes, Pete Elderfield (basses), Don Lawson, Benny Goodman (drums).

Don Rendell Quintet (Tempo EP EXA 20) 1955
Don Rendell (tenor), Ronnie Ross (baritone), Damian Robinson (piano), Sammy Stokes (bass), Benny Goodman (drums).

Tenorama (Nixa NJL 4) 1956
Don Rendell (tenor), Damian Robinson (piano), Pete Elderfield (bass), Don Lawson (drums).

Jazz Britannia (one side only) (MGM EP 615) 1956
Don Rendell (tenor), Damian Robinson (piano), Pete Elderfield (bass), Don Lawson (drums).

Introducing (Nixa NJL 7) 1957
Kenny Wheeler, Bert Courtley (trumpets), Don Rendell (tenor), Ronnie Ross (alto/baritone), Ken Moule (piano), Pete Blannin, Arthur Watts (basses), Don Lawson (drums).

Doggin' Around (Nixa NIE 1044)   1957
Kenny Wheeler, Bert Courtley (trumpets), Don Rendell (tenor), Ronnie
Ross(alto/baritone), Eddie Harvey (trombone/piano), Kenny Napper (bass),
Phil Seamen (drums).

Playtime (Decca LK 4265)   1958
Bert Courtley (trumpet), Ronnie Ross (alto/baritone), Don Rendell (tenor),
Eddie Harvey (trombone/piano), Pete Blannin (bass), Andy White (drums).

The Jazz Committee (Decca DFE 6587)   1959
Bert Courtley (trumpet), Don Rendell (tenor), Eddie Harvey (trombone/
piano), Pete Blannin (bass), Jackie Dougan (drums).

Roarin' (Jazzland JLP 51)   1961
Don Rendell (tenor), Graham Bond (alto), Johnny Burch (piano), Tony
Archer (bass), Phil Kinorra (drums).

Spacewalk (Columbia SCX 6491)   1971
Don Rendell (soprano/tenor/flute/alto flute), Stan Robinson (tenor/clarinet/
flute), Jack Thorncroft (bass), Trevor Tomkins (drums), Peter Shade
(vibes/flute).

24. DON RENDELL–IAN CARR QUINTET
Shades Of Blue (Columbia 33SX 1733)   1965
Don Rendell (tenor/soprano), Ian Carr (trumpet/flugelhorn), Colin Purbrook
(piano), Dave Green (bass), Trevor Tomkins (drums).

Dusk Fire (Columbia SX 6064)   1966
Don Rendell (tenor/soprano/flute/clarinet, Ian Carr (trumpet/flugelhorn),
Michael Garrick (piano), Dave Green (bass), Trevor Tomkins (drums).

Phase III (Columbia SX 6214)   1968
Don Rendell (tenor/soprano/flute), Ian Carr (trumpet/flugelhorn), Michael
Garrick (piano), Dave Green (bass), Trevor Tomkins (drums).

Live (Columbia SCX 6316)   1969
Don Rendell (tenor/soprano/clarinet/flute), Ian Carr (trumpet/flugelhorn),
Dave Green (bass), Michael Garrick (piano), Trevor Tomkins (drums).

Change-Is (Columbia SCX 6368)   1969
Don Rendell (flute/tenor/soprano), Ian Carr (trumpet/flugelhorn), Michael
Garrick (piano/harpsichord), Dave Green (bass), Trevor Tomkins (drums),
Mike Pyne (piano), Jeff Clyne (bass), Stan Robinson, (tenor/clarinet), Guy
Warren (talking drums/bells/maraccas).

25. HOWARD RILEY
Discussions (Opportunity 2500)   1967
Howard Riley (piano), Barry Guy (bass), Jon Hiseman (drums).

Angle (CBS Realm 52669)   1968/1969
Howard Riley (piano), Barry Guy (bass), Alan Jackson (drums), Barbara
Thompson (flute).

The Day Will Come (CBS 64077)   1970
Howard Riley (piano), Barry Guy (bass), Alan Jackson (drums).

Flight (Turtle 301)   1970
Howard Riley (piano), Barry Guy (bass), Tony Oxley (drums/amplified percussion).

26. FRANK RICOTTI
Our Point of View (CBS 52668)   1969
Frank Ricotti (vibes/alto), Chris Spedding (guitar), Chris Laurence (bass),
Bryan Spring (drums).

Ricotti and Albuquerque (Pegasus 2)   1971
Frank Ricotti (vibes/alto/percussion), Michael Albuquerque (vocals/ guitar),
John Taylor (piano), Chris Laurence (bass), Trevor Tomkins (drums).

27. RAY RUSSELL
Turn Circle (CBS 52586)   1968
Ray Russell (guitar), Roy Fry (piano), Ron Matthewson (bass), Alan Rushton
(drums).

Dragon Hill (CBS 52663)   1969
Ray Russell (guitar), Roy Fry (piano), Alan Rushton (drums), Ron Matthewson
(bass), Harry Beckett (trumpet/flugelhorn), Bud Parkes (trumpet), Lyn
Dobson (tenor), Donald Beichtol (trombone).

Rites And Rituals (CBS 64075)   1970
Ray Russell (guitar), Daryl Runswick (bass), Harry Beckett (trumpet), Tony
Roberts (tenor/flutes), Nick Evans (trombone), Alan Rushton (drums).

Rock Workshop (CBS 64075)   1970
Bud Parkes, Harry Beckett (trumpets), Tony Roberts, Bob Downes (tenors),
Derek Wadsworth (trombone), Brian Miller (keyboards), Daryl Runswick
(bass guitar), Alan Rushton (drums), Robin Jones (congas), Ray Russell (guitar), Laurie Baker (synthesizer), Alan Greed, Alan Harvey (vocals).

The Very Last Time (CBS 64394)   1971
Bud Parkes, Harry Beckett (trumpets), Tony Roberts, Bob Downes (tenors),
Derek Wadsworth (trombone), Brian Miller (keyboards), Daryl Runswick
(bass guitar), Alan Rushton (drums), Tony Uter (congas), Ray Russell (guitar),
Alan Greed (vocals).

Live At The ICA (RCA SF 8214)   1971
Ray Russell (guitar), Tony Roberts (tenor/flutes), Harry Beckett
(trumpet/flugelhorn), Daryl Runswick (bass), Alan Rushton (drums).

Running Man (RCA Neon NE11)   1972
Ray Russell (guitar/bass guitar), Alan Rushton (drums), Alan Greed (vocals),
Harry Beckett (trumpet/flugelhorn), Gary Windo (tenor).

Secret Asylum (Black Lion 2 460 207)   1973
Ray Russell (guitar), Daryl Runswick (bass guitar), Alan Rushton (drums),
Harry Beckett (trumpet/flugelhorn), Gary Windo (tenor).

28. ALAN SKIDMORE

Jazz In Britain 1968/69 (one side) (Decca ECS 2114)   1969
Alan Skidmore (tenor), Kenny Wheeler (trumpet), John Taylor (piano),
Harry Miller (bass), Tony Oxley (drums).

Once Upon A Time (Decca SDN 11)   1969
Alan Skidmore (tenor), Kenny Wheeler (trumpet/flugelhorn), John Taylor
(piano), Harry Miller (bass), Tony Oxley (drums).

TCB (Philips 63060)   1970
Alan Skidmore (tenor), Malcolm Griffiths (trombone), John Taylor (piano),
Chris Laurence (bass), Tony Levin (drums).

29. JOHN STEVENS / TREVOR WATTS

Challenge: Spontaneous Music Ensemble (Eyemark EMPL 1002)   1966
Kenny Wheeler (trumpet/flugelhorn), John Stevens (drums), Paul Rutherford
(trombone), Bruce Cale, Jeff Clyne (basses), Trevor Watts (reeds).

Springboard (Polydor 545 007)   1966
Jeff Clyne (bass), Ian Carr (trumpet/flugelhorn), Trevor Watts (reeds), John
Stevens (drums).

Karyobin: Spontaneous Music Ensemble (Island ILPS 9079)   1968
Kenny Wheeler (trumpet/flugelhorn), Dave Holland (bass), Evan Parker

(reeds), Derek Bailey (guitar), John Stevens (drums).

Oliv: SME (Marmalade 608008)   1969
Trevor Watts (reeds), John Stevens (drums), Kenny Wheeler (trumpet/ flugel-
horn), Derek Bailey (guitar), Pete Lemer (piano), Johnny Dyani (bass), Maggie
Nichols, Carolann Nichols, Pepi Lemer (vocals).

Prayer For Peace: Amalgam (Transatlantic 196)   1969
John Stevens (drums), Trevor Watts (reeds), Jeff Clyne (bass), Barry Guy
(bass).

The Source: SME (Tangent TNGS 107)   1970
Trevor Watts, Ray Warleigh, Brian Smith (reeds), Kenny Wheeler,
(trumpet/flugelhorn), Bob Nordern, Chris Pyne (trombones), Mike Pyne
(piano), Ron Matthewson, Marcio Mattos (basses), John Stevens (drums).

SME For CND For Peace And You To Share (A Records)   1970
John Stevens (drums), Trevor Watts (reeds), with a workshop group.

Birds Of A Feather: SME (BYG 529023)   1971
Trevor Watts (reeds), John Stevens (drums), Ron Herman (bass), Julie
Tippetts (vocals/guitar).

So What Do You Think?: SME (Tangent TGS 116)   1971
John Stevens (drums), Trevor Watts (reeds), Kenny Wheeler (trumpet/flugel-
horn), Dave Holland (bass/cello), Derek Bailey (guitar).

Bobby Bradford Plus SME (Freedom SLP 40110/1)   1971
Bobby Bradford (trumpet), John Stevens (drums), Trevor Watts, (reeds), Ron
Herman (bass), Julie Tippetts (vocals/guitar), Bob Nordern (trombone).

30. JOHN SURMAN
John Surman (Deram DML/SML 1030)   1968
Harry Beckett, Kenny Wheeler (trumpets), Malcolm Griffiths, Paul
Rutherford (trombones), Tony Bennellick (French horn), John Surman, Mike
Osborne (saxophones), Russ Henderson (piano), Harry Miller, Dave Holland
(basses), Alan Jackson, Stirling Betancourt (drums), Erroll Philip (percussion).

How Many Clouds Can You See (Deram SML R 10 45)   1969
Harry Beckett, Dave Holdsworth (trumpets), Malcolm Griffiths, Chris Pyne
(trombones), George Smith (tuba), John Surman, Mike Osborne, Alan
Skidmore, John Warren (saxophones), John Taylor (piano), Harry Miller,
Barre Phillips (basses), Alan Jackson, Tony Oxley (drums).

Alors!! (Futura Records GER 12)   1970
John Surman (baritone/soprano/bass clarinet), Michel Portal (alto/bass
clarinet), Barre Phillips (bass), Stu Martin (drums), Jean-Pierre Drouet
(percussion).

The Trio (Dawn DNLS 3006)   1970
John Surman (baritone/soprano/bass clarinet), Barre Phillips (bass), Stu
Martin (drums).

Tales Of The Algonquin (see under John Warren).

Conflagration (Dawn DNLS 3022)   1971
Harry Beckett, Kenny Wheeler, Marc Charig (trumpets), Malcolm Griffiths,
Nick Evans (trombones), Mike Osborne, Stan Sulzman, Alan Skidmore, John
Surman (saxophones), Chick Corea, John Taylor (piano), Dave Holland,
Barre Phillips (basses), Stu Martin, John Marshall (drums).

Westering Home (Island Records HELP 10)   1972
John Surman (various instruments).

Morning Glory (Island Records ILPS 9237)   1973
John Surman (soprano/bass clarinet), Malcolm Griffiths (trombone), John
Taylor (piano/electric piano), Terje Rypdal (guitar), Chris Laurence (bass),
John Marshall (drums).

31. JOHN TAYLOR
Pause And Think Again (Turtle TUR 302)   1971
John Taylor (piano), Kenny Wheeler (trumpet), Chris Pyne (trombone), Stan
Sulzman (alto), Chris Laurence (bass), Tony Levin (drums), John Surman
(soprano), Norma Winstone (voice).

32. MIKE TAYLOR
Pendulum (Columbia SX 6042)   1965
Mike Taylor (piano), Tony Reeves (bass), Jon Hiseman (drums), Dave
Tomlin (soprano/tenor).

Trio (Columbia SX 6137)   1966
Mike Taylor (piano), Ron Rubin, Jack Bruce (basses), Jon Hiseman (drums).

33. KEITH TIPPETT
You Are Here: I Am There (Polydor 2384004)   1969
Marc Charig (cornet), Elton Dean (alto), Nick Evans (trombone), Jeff Clyne
(bass/bass guitar), Alan Jackson (drums/glockenspiel), Keith Tippett
(piano/electric piano).

Dedicated To You But You Weren't Listening (Vertigo 6360024)   1970
Keith Tippett (piano), Elton Dean (alto/saxello), Marc Charig (trumpet), Nick
Evans (trombone), Roy Babbington (bass guitar), Bryan Spring, Robert Wyatt,
Phil Howard (drums), Tony Uter (congas/cowbells), Neville Whitehead
(bass), Gary Boyle (guitar).

Septober Energy: Centipede (RCA Neon NE 9)   1971
Fifty-piece Orchestra.

Blueprint (RCA Victor SF 8290)   1972
Keith Tippett (piano), Roy Babbington (bass guitar), Frank Perry (percussion),
Julie Tippetts (vocals/guitar/recorder/mandolin), Keith Bailey (percussion).

34. STAN TRACEY
Showcase (Vogue VA 160130)   1958
Stan Tracey (piano), Kenny Napper (bass), Phil Seamen, Ronnie Verrell
(drums), Johnny Hawkesworth (bass).

Little Klunk (Vogue VA 160155)   1959
Stan Tracey (piano), Kenny Napper (bass), Phil Seamen (drums).

The New Departures Quartet (Transatlantic TRA 134)   1964
Stan Tracey (piano), Bobby Wellins (tenor), Jeff Clyne (bass), Laurie Morgan
(drums).

Under Milk Wood (Columbia 33SX1774)   1965
Stan Tracey (piano), Bobby Wellins (tenor), Jeff Clyne (bass), Jackie Dougan
(drums).

Alice In Jazzland (Columbia SX 6051)   1966
Kenny Baker, Eddie Blair, Ian Hamer, Les Condon (trumpets), Keith
Christie, Chris Smith, Wally Smith (trombones), Alan Branscombe, Ronnie
Baker (altos), Ronnie Scott, Bobby Wellins (tenors), Harry Klein (baritone),
Jeff Clyne (bass), Ronnie Stevenson (drums), Tubby Hayes (tenor), Kenny
Wheeler (trumpet/flugelhorn), Stan Tracey (piano).

In Person (Columbia SX 6124)   1967
Stan Tracey (piano).

With Love From Jazz (Columbia SCX 6205)   1968
Stan Tracey (piano), Bobby Wellins (tenor), Dave Green, Lennie Bush
(bass), Jackie Dougan, Ronnie Stevenson (drums).

Latin American Caper (Columbia SCX 6358)   1969
Kenny Baker, Derek Watkins, Eddie Blair, Les Condon (trumpets), Keith
Christie, Morris Pratt, Bobby Lambe (trombones), Chris Taylor, Roy Willox,
Ray Swinfield (flutes), Ronnie Chamberlain, Don Rendell, Derek Collins
(clarinets), Alan Branscombe (vibes/marimba), Lennie Bush, Dave Green
(basses), Barry Morgan (drums/Latin American percussion), Denis Lopez,
Stuart Gordon (Latin American percussion), Stan Tracey (piano).

We Love You Madly (Columbia SX6320)   1969
Stan Tracey (piano), Acker Bilk (clarinet), Ian Carr (flugelhorn), Tony Coe
(tenor sax), Joe Harriott (alto sax), Don Rendell (soprano), Derek Watkins,
Paul Tongay, Kenny Baker, Eddie Blair, Les Condon (trumpets), Keith
Christie, Don Lusher, Chris Pyne, Bobby Lambe, Chris Smith (trombones),
Lennie Bush (bass), Barry Morgan (drums).

Free 'N' One (Columbia SCX 6385)   1970
Stan Tracey (piano), Peter King (alto), Dave Green (bass), Bryan Spring
(drums).

Seven Ages Of Man (Columbia SCX 6413)   1970
Stan Tracey (piano), Derek Watkins, Tony Fisher, Henry Shaw, Greg Bowen
(trumpets), Keith Christie, Chris Pyne, Mike Gibbs (trombones), Peter King,
Dennis Walton (altos), Tony Coe (tenor/clarinet), Alan Skidmore (tenor),
Ronnie Ross (baritone), Frank Ricotti (vibes/clarinet), Dave Green (bass),
Bryan Spring (drums).

Perspectives (Columbia SCX 6485)   1972
Stan Tracey (piano), Dave Green (bass), Bryan Spring (drums).

35. RAY WARLEIGH
Ray Warleigh's First Album (Philips SBL 7881)   1968
Ray Warleigh (alto/flute), Gordon Beck (piano), Dave Goldberg (guitar),
Kenny Napper (bass), Ronnie Stevenson, Terry Cox (drums), with 16-piece
orchestra led by Ralph Elman and Reg Leopold, arranged and conducted by
Harry South and Derek Warne.

36. GUY WARREN OF GHANA
Afro-Jazz (Columbia SX 6340)   1968
Guy Warren (drums/congas/bamboo flute/talking drums/African xylophone),
Don Rendell (tenor/soprano), Ian Carr (trumpet/flugelhorn), Trevor Tomkins
(drums), Dave Green (bass), Amancio D'Silva (guitar), Michael Garrick
(piano).

The African Soundz (Regal Zonophone SLRZ 1031)   1972
Guy Warren (drums/percussion/African drums), Amancio D'Silva (guitar),
Dick Heckstall-Smith (reeds), Les Phillips (guitar).

37. JOHN WARREN
Tales Of The Algonquin with John Surman (Deram SML 1094)   1971
Martin Drover, Kenny Wheeler, Harry Beckett (trumpets/flugelhorns),
Malcolm Griffiths, Ed Harvey, Danny Almark (trombones), Mike Osborne
(alto/clarinet), Stan Sulzman (alto/soprano/flute), Alan Skidmore
(tenor/flute/alto flute), John Surman (baritone/soprano), John Warren (bari-
tone/flute), John Taylor (piano), Harry Miller, Barre Phillips (basses), Alan
Jackson, Stu Martin (drums/percussion).

38. MIKE WESTBROOK
Celebration (Deram SML 1013)   1967
Mike Westbrook (piano), John Surman, Mike Osborne, Dave Chambers,
Bernie Living (saxophones), Dave Holdsworth (trumpet), Malcolm Griffiths,
Dave Perrotet (trombones), George Smith (tuba), Harry Miller (bass), Alan
Jackson (drums).

Release (Deram AML 1031)   1968
Mike Westbrook (piano), John Surman, Mike Osborne, George Khan,
Bernie Living (saxophones), Dave Holdsworth (trumpet), Malcolm Griffiths,
Paul Rutherford (trombones), Harry Miller (bass), Alan Jackson (drums).

Marching Song Vols. I and II (Deram SML 1047/8)   1969
Mike Westbrook (piano), Dave Holdsworth, Kenny Wheeler, Greg Bowen,
Tony Fisher, Henry Lowther, Ronnie Hughes (trumpets), Malcolm Griffiths,
Paul Rutherford, Mike Gibbs, Eddie Harvey (trombones), Tony Bennellick
(French horn), Martin Fry, George Smith (tubas), John Surman, Mike
Osborne, Bernie Living, Alan Skidmore, George Khan, John Warren, Brian
Smith (saxophones), Harry Miller, Barre Phillips, Chris Laurence (basses),
Alan Jackson, John Marshall (drums).

Love Songs (Deram SML 1069)   1970
Norma Winstone (vocals), Mike Westbrook (piano), Dave Holdsworth (trumpet), Malcolm Griffiths, Paul Rutherford (trombones), Mike Osborne, George
Khan, John Warren (saxophones), Chris Spedding (guitar), Harry Miller
(bass/bass guitar), Alan Jackson (drums).

Metropolis (RCA Neon NE 10)   1971
Mike Westbrook (piano), Nigel Carter, Kenny Wheeler, Harry Beckett,
Henry Lowther, Dave Holdsworth (trumpets), Malcolm Griffiths, Paul
Rutherford, Paul Nieman, Derek Wadsworth, Geoff Perkins (trombones),

Mike Osborne, Ray Warleigh, Alan Skidmore, George Khan, John Warren (saxophones), John Taylor (electric piano), Gary Boyle (guitar), Harry Miller (bass), Chris Laurence (bass guitar), Alan Jackson, John Marshall (drums), Norma Winstone (vocals).

Tyger: A Celebration Of William Blake (RCA Red Seal SER 5612)   1971
Mike Westbrook (piano), Fiachra Trench, John Mitchell (organ/piano), Alan Jackson (drums), Gary Boyle (guitar), Dave Wintour (bass guitar), George Khan (saxophone), Malcolm Griffiths (trombone), Dave Holdsworth (trumpet).

Solid Gold Cadillac (RCA SF 8311)   1972
Phil Minton (vocals), George Khan (saxophone), Malcolm Griffiths (trombone), Mike Westbrook (electric piano), Fiachra Trench (piano/organ), Roy Babbington (bass/bass guitar), Alan Jackson (drums), Chris Spedding (guitar).

Mike Westbrook Live (Cadillac SGC 1001)   1972
George Khan (electric sax/tenor/flute), Gary Boyle (guitar), Mike Westbrook (electric piano/harmonium), Butch Potter (bass guitar/flute), Alan Jackson (drums/alto).

39. KENNY WHEELER
Windmill Tilter (Fontana STL 5494)   1968
Derek Watkins, Henry Lowther, Henry Shaw, Les Condon (trumpets), Kenny Wheeler (trumpet/flugelhorn), John Dankworth, Tony Roberts, Ray Swinfield, Tony Coe (reeds), Chris Pyne, Mike Gibbs (trombones), Dick Hart, Alfie Reece (tubas), Dave Holland (bass), John McLaughlin (guitar), Alan Branscombe, Bob Cornford (pianos), Tristan Fry (vibes/bongos), John Spooner (drums).

(untitled) (as yet unissued)   1973
Greg Bowen, Ian Hamer, Dave Hancock (trumpets), Kenny Wheeler (trumpet/flugelhorn), Dave Horler, Keith Christie, Jim Wilson, Chris Pyne, Bobby Lambe (trombones), Duncan Lamont, Mike Osborne (reeds), Alfie Reece (tuba), John Taylor, Alan Branscombe (pianos), Ron Matthewson (bass), Tony Oxley (drums), Norma Winstone (vocals).

40. NORMA WINSTONE
Edge Of Time (Argo DA 148)   1971
Henry Lowther, Kenny Wheeler (trumpets/flugelhorns), Malcolm Griffiths, Chris Pyne (trombones), Paul Rutherford (trombone/euphonium), Alan Skidmore, Mike Osborne, Art Themen (reeds), Frank Ricotti (vibes), John Taylor (piano/electric piano), Chris Laurence (bass), Tony Levin (drums), Gary Boyle (guitar), Norma Winstone (voice)

INDEX

OTHER JAZZ BOOKS
FROM NORTHWAY

FORTHCOMING JAZZ BOOKS FROM NORTHWAY

Mike Hennessey
The Little Giant: a biography of Johnny Griffin

Derek Ansell
Workout – The Music of Hank Mobley

Chris Searle
*Forward Groove: Jazz and the Real World
from Louis Armstrong to Gilad Atzmon*

Graham Collier
The Jazz Composer

Peter King
an autobiography

Ron Rubin
musical limericks

www.northwaybooks.com